val d isere

espace killy

first edition 2004

written and edited by
Michael Kayson & Isobel Rostron

Qanuk Publishing & Design Ltd
www.snowmole.com

the snowmole guide to **val d'isère espace killy**
first edition 2004

published by Qanuk Publishing & Design Ltd
45 Mysore Road London SW11 5RY

printed by Craftprint, Singapore

ISBN 0-9545739-9-4

A catalogue record of this book is available from the British Library.

contents

how to use the guide

How much you enjoy your winter holiday depends on a variety of things. Some you cannot influence - you can't guarantee sunshine, good snow, or your flight landing on time... but most things should be within your control. With the majority of ski holidays lasting just a week or less, you don't want to waste time trying to find a good restaurant, or struggling with an overgrown piste map. The snowmole guides are designed with 2 purposes in mind: to save you time by providing essential information on the operation of the resort, and to help you to make the most of your time by giving insight into every aspect of your stay.

The guide is not intended to be read from cover to cover. After the introduction to the resort, the guide is split into 4 distinct sections - getting started, the skiing, the resort and the a-z - so you can dip into the information you need when you need it. Some information will be useful to you beforehand, some while you are in resort and some while you are on the mountain.

getting started   deals with the basics: how to get to the resort, how to get around once you're there, and your options when buying your lift pass, renting equipment and booking lessons or mountain guides.

the skiing   gives an overview of the mountains and the ski area, information on the off-piste, and a breakdown for beginners, intermediates, experts, boarders and non-skiers. The ski domain has been divided into digestible chunks and for each there is a detailed description of the pistes and lifts.

the resort   covers the best of the rest of your holiday: a series of reviews on where to eat, where to play, what to do when skiing isn't an option, facilities for children and tips for seasonnaires. Those places that in our opinion deserve a lengthier review are written as a 'feature'.

the a-z   comprises a list of tour operators, a directory of contact details (telephone numbers and website addresses) and information from accidents to weather, a glossary of terms used in this guide and in skiing in general, and an index to help navigate your way around the guide.

how to use the maps

The guide also features a number of maps, designed and produced specifically for snowmole. While the information they contain is as accurate as possible, some omissions have been made for the sake of clarity.

route maps
show the journey to the resort from the UK, or from relevant airports or the roads within the area surrounding the resort.

resort maps
for the resort as a whole (showing pedestrianised zones, main buildings, train lines, car paaks and road names) and individual maps showing by type the places we review.

ski maps
each individual area has its own contoured map. These show details such as the lifts, pistes and mountain restaurants. The contours have been mapped to fit an A6 page - few ski areas are perfect rectangles. They are accurate only in relation to the pistes they depict and should not be used for navigation. Pistes are shown only in their approximate path - to make the maps as user-friendly as possible some twists and turns have been omitted. The ski maps are grouped together at the back of the book to make them easy to find and refer to - even with gloves on. There is an overview map on the inside back cover that shows the entire ski domain and how the individual ski maps fit together. The back cover has a flap, which is useful as a page marker for the individual ski maps. In the chapter on the skiing the overview map is reproduced in miniature alongside the descriptions of the individual sectors.

explanation of icons

review headers

name — price rating

relevant icons

☎ 0479 055578
🕐 7:30-10:30am, 4pm-10:30am
🍴 traditional savoyarde

p107 b4 — map details: page number, grid reference & map cutout showing type and number reference

basic details

- ☎ - telephone number
- 📠 - fax number
- @ - email address
- W^3 - website address
- 🛏 - number of beds
- 📧 - office address
- 🕐 - opening hours
- 🍴 - food type

ski school

- ⛷ - ski lessons
- 🏂 - snowboard lessons
- 🧍 - child-specific lessons
- ♿ - disabled skiing
- ⛷ - specialist courses
- **G** - guides available

hotel

- 🥾 - on-site rental store
- 🚌 - shuttle bus

others

- 🍴 - food available
- 🎵 - live music
- 📺 - tv
- 🎧 - internet station(s)
- 🍸 - bar
- • - terrace

resort maps

buildings

- 🛈 - tourist office
- 📋 - lift pass office
- PO - post office
- 🛒 - supermarket
- 🎬 - cinema
- ✝ - church

travel specific

- **P** - parking
- **P̂** - covered parking
- Ⓑ - bus stop
- 🚌 - route specific bus stop

commerce colour coding

- ⬜ - restaurant (local cuisine)
- ⬛ - restaurant
- ⬜ - cafe
- ⬛ - take-away
- ⬛ - bar
- ⬛ - nightclub
- ⬛ - hotel

route maps

 - train line & station

 - main road & town

 - country borders

 - motorway & town

 - airport

 graphic design by Ranuk Publishing & Design Ltd

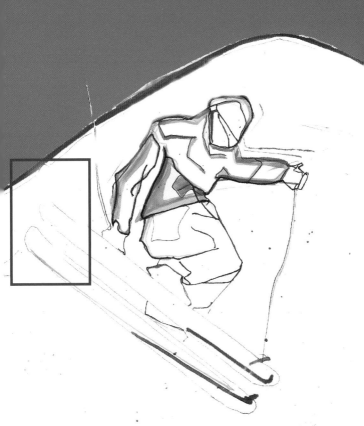

introducing val d'isère

overview

If the English were to lay claim to some corner of a foreign mountain, Val d'Isère would be it. It is well documented as being the most English part of the Alps, but those that go there are not just xenophobic tourists. Arguably as expensive as Courchevel 1850, if you can afford it Val provides a haven of high-class restaurants, high-end accommodation and high-street shopping, and the Espace Killy offers a slickly maintained area of broad pistes and steep powder.

Val is a superb holiday destination, its only real downside being that it knows it. It is not perfect: the tourist office can be less than enthusiastic, and though an

attractive place it lacks the chocolate-box charm of resorts like Verbier or Zermatt - but arrogance and modern glitz are overshadowed by fantastic skiing, an excellent lift system, and an all-night night life. As long as you bring your bank balance you will enjoy every second of your stay.

The centre of Val d'Isère consists essentially of 1 long street, about as far up the Isèran valley as you can get in winter. Along that street and its few tributaries almost every commerce is either a ski shop, a clothes shop, a bar or a restaurant - which means that walking around town is a window-shopper's heaven, and that no matter where you are you're never far from what you're looking for.

Though now inescapably an out-and-out tourist spot, Val was a town long before people thought of racing down snow with wood strapped to their feet. These days the old village is somewhat hidden by bright lights and big hotels, but a few steps south of the bustle there remains a beautiful and relatively calm couple of streets that show what Val was before the skiing boom. There's not much there now - indeed there wasn't much there then, but if you want to escape the bustle for a few minutes you could do worse than venture back in time to the Vieux Village, so 'vieux' that some parts of the church standing there date back to the 11th Century. For the more modern parts of the resort the nickname 'Val de Sloane Square' is as deserved as it is well known - that is to say, if you go during the English school holidays you are likely to share your trip with a decent slice of the English upper-middle class. When the kids are at school and the prices come down, however, there is little to distinguish Val's tourist population from that of other ski resorts.

Surprisingly, the English make up little over 30% of the population at peak - though you may not believe it they are still outnumbered by the French. There are plenty of Dutch, a healthy dose of Scandinavians and other Europeans in addition to the considerable French contingent, particularly affluent Parisians. And as with many of the better-known European resorts, Val's popularity is also growing amongst the Russian nouveau riche.

11

Most of Val's accommodation falls into the mid-range bracket. There are lots of pleasant places to stay, along with a few very, very nice ones (and a few dingy ones). Val has many chalets, a handful of chalet hotels, a number of hotels proper, a sprinkling of apartments and all the shades of grey: everything from superior luxury in the Barmes de l'Ours to seasonnaires sleeping in camper vans.

Val d'Isère can lay claim to some excellent evening entertainment. From bars with theme nights that

snapshot

highs...
great on-piste skiing for all levels
great off-piste skiing for all levels
good lift network
a party town
lots of english

and lows
lots of english
long transfer from the airports
can be very busy on the slopes and in resort
can sometimes feel cliquey and pretentious
not cheap

sound (and are) like student parties, to quiet evenings with sofas and cigars, there is a diversity of attractions that allows you to choose your poison. And while many bars target the various types of English tourist there are also places to escape your native language if you wish to do so.

Eating out in Val is not cheap. Unless you're happy with pizza and chips, your evening meal will turn out a few Euros more pricey than in your average ski resort - but then this is not your average ski resort. Nowhere is Val's self-awareness more prevalent than in some of the mid-range restaurants that churn out fondue and charge the earth - but if you pick the right spot, filling your stomach will be as satisfying as any other part of your holiday.

The combined ski area of Val d'Isère and Tignes is named after Val's most famous son, Jean-Claude Killy, who although born near Paris was raised in Val, and who dominated world ski racing in the 1960s. The 'Espace' stretches from the Pissaillas Glacier in the north (home of Val's summer skiing) to Les Brevières on one side of Tignes and the Grande Motte (home of Tignes' summer skiing) on the other. It boasts some 99 lifts providing access to around 300kms of pistes and a huge skiable area of about 25000 hectares. Access from Val to the ski area is excellent - with no fewer than 8 points from where to start your ascent - 4 from Val, 3 in La Daille, plus the Fornet cable car.

12

The Espace Killy is boldly marketed as 'the most beautiful ski area in the world' - a highly subjective and somewhat irrelevant claim that would struggle to argue its case when confronted with places like Chamonix or Zermatt. But skin-deep aestheticism aside, the Espace Killy has a huge amount to offer. Though it may sound small compared to the 600kms clocked up by the 3 Vallées a little way back down the road, the stats are deceptive. It is in fact a very large area with wide and rolling pistes ideal for beginners and

intermediates, a number of nerve-testing blacks, including the well-known Face and a vast expanse off-piste, much of which is lift accessed. Every level of ability is catered for, from debutant to extreme skier, and within a week's holiday you will not be short of challenge or variety.

The Isèran valley has, to an extent, its own weather system, and in general the micro-climate is perfectly suited to ski holidays. As with anywhere it is subject to the occasional blip, but generally Val gets good snow and lots of sunshine - and the result is lots of people.

temperatures

It's fairly easy to generalise temperatures - December and January are usually the coldest months, with things warming up gradually through February, March and April. When you are in resort, don't be fooled by appearances - it will often be colder when there is a cloudless, blue sky than when snow is falling. Temperatures can range from -15°C at ground level on the coldest days to as high as 20°C later on in the season when the sun is shining.

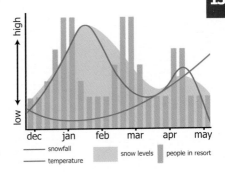

snowfall
temperature
snow levels
people in resort

snowfall

The Espace Killy has an excellent snow record, and though of course the timing of snowfall varies greatly from year to year, the Isèran valley commands its own weather system which can mean good early season coverage even when nearby areas like Paradiski and the 3 Vallées have little.

volume of people in resort

Val has a reasonably sized year-round population (and a busy summer season) - so there is life in the town at all times. The main pedestrian areas are closely enough knit that it always feels quite busy, and in peak season almost everywhere (including the pistes) will be full. As with anywhere else volume fluctuates according to holiday times, and Val gets a good contribution from French families throughout the 4 weeks of the staggered French February half-terms. Val's inaccessibility means there are few weekenders - either from England or France. Combine that with the two-day transfer split and you've got relatively underpopulated slopes most weekends - making it a good place for a Thursday to Monday jaunt, if you don't mind the long transfer from your arrival airport.

Ski resorts are as varied as DNA. But what makes Val d'Isère Val d'Isère? To have a quintessential time...

save face
You will inevitably see - and more than likely ski - the Face at some point during

your stay. The site of the 1992 Olympic men's downhill, it runs almost the length of the Olmpique cable car, from which the entire run is visible. It is the most direct route back to Val from the Bellevarde ski area. But its lures are the downfall (literally) of many skiers - it is not an easy run, largely thanks to it being littered with skiers who thought it sounded like a good idea but don't like how steep it is when they get there. This is not to say that you should't try it if you want to - but maybe not on the first day. Give your legs a chance to get back in shape, and leave the Face for the middle of the week when you're skiing like a champion again.

get first tracks
Whether you are more inclined to small steps or giant leaps, the Espace Killy will

not disappoint those with a passion for the soft stuff. Even if you've never been off-piste before and don't see what the fuss is about, this is the place to get your first taste. A huge unpisted area and an excellent snow record combine to give you pretty good odds on seeing sugar at some point during your stay - and there's enough gentle terrain for even the most timid skier to have a stab at blazing a new trail.

show your true colours
It is easy to make assumptions about people who spend their winter holiday in Val d'Isère - the restaurants are pricey, the shops are pricey, and the chances are that even if you have never been there you've met (or heard) someone who has been, and who has been to Banana's or Dick's one time too many. But behind the scenes the post-ski culture has as many shades of grey as there are shades of grey - yes you can drink vodka

freestyles to your heart's delight, or toffee vodkas (though no vodka red bull), but if you look around a bit you will find somewhere that suits you no matter if your taste is for cocktail bars, comfy sofa bars, chilled champagne bars or fat cigar bars.

pull a sickie

Sometimes, the idea of working 5 days in a row is all too much. The evolution of the 24-hour flu bug means that these days it is relatively easy to organise a day off to catch up on sleep, or do a bit of shopping, or spend some quality time with the TV... if you don't like the sound of 5 days of work, 6 days of snow-based exercise probably sounds pretty taxing too. Val d'Isère has no shortage of alternative pastimes - so blame the cold weather and spend a day wandering lazily around town, buying clothes and drinking hot chocolate.

speak the lingo

Part of the joy of going abroad is the opportunity to learn about foreign cultures, to get away from your well-nutured English preconceptions. Language is a fundamental part of the identity of any community, and the ability to communicate with the locals in their native tongue is crucial to being able to fit in. So before you leave for Val, get yourself down to the local language school and brush up on your RP English.

stop for lunch

There are plenty of good places to take a break and fill your stomach over the lunch hour. What you may be interested to learn, however, is that from every single mountain restaurant on the Val side of the Espace Killy, you can ski down without having to take a single lift. You may have to sit on a bus when you get to the bottom, but if you find a good spot in the sunshine and feel inclined to get yourself outside a few glasses of vin chaud, you can do so safe in the knowledge that at closing time all you have to do is strap on your skis and point yourself down the hill.

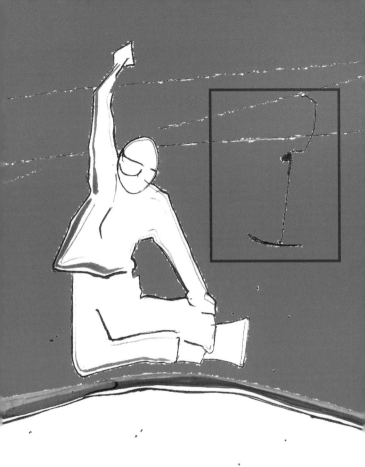

getting started

Once you know you want to go to Val d'Isère, you need to decide how you want to get there. Traditionally, most skiing holidays are booked though travel agents or tour operators, but with the advent of cheap flights, DIY holidays are becoming more popular. There are pros and cons to both.

18 package

The theory behind package holidays is that all you should have to think about is getting from the top of the slopes to the bottom. The core of every package deal is convenience - though it comes wrapped in all kinds of paper. Ski companies fall into 2 types: large mainstream operators, and smaller more specialist ones. The mainstream brand offers ready-made holidays, where everything is already planned and you take it or leave it. Trips with smaller companies can be more expensive, but tend to be more flexible and many tailor the trip to your exact requirements. Alternatively, if you don't want to be restricted to a single operator, a travel agent will have access to a selection of holidays offered by several companies.

Mainstream companies only run week-long trips, from Saturday to Saturday or Sunday to Sunday - giving you 6 days on the slopes and 7 nights in (or on) the town. They charter their own **flights** - making the holiday cheaper - but you have little option as to when or from where you travel. Smaller ski

companies give you greater choice - many specialise in long weekends for the 'money-rich, time-poor' market, with departures on Thursday evenings and returns on Monday evenings. This gives you 4 days skiing for 2 days off work... but the real advantage is their use of scheduled flights, so you can pick the airport, airline, and when you travel.

With a mainstream company, your **transfer** to resort will be by coach, with others who have booked through the same company. You may have to wait for other flights, and on the way there may be stop-offs in other resorts or at other accommodation before your own. Because you're travelling at the weekend the journey tends to take longer. With a smaller company you may transfer by coach, minibus, taxi, or car depending on how much you've paid and the size of your group. And if you arrive mid-week, the transfers tend to be quicker.

What your **accommodation** is depends entirely on whom you book with. Different companies have deals with different hotels, some specialise in chalets... the limiting factor is what's in the brochure - though if you want to stay in a particular hotel, a more specialist company may try to organise it for you.

In **resort** some companies offer a drop-off and pick-up service from the lifts. But the main benefit of a package holiday is the resort rep. From the moment you arrive to the moment you leave, there is someone whose job it is to ensure your holiday goes smoothly... or that's the theory. More than likely your rep will sort out lift passes and equipment rental. Some will organise evening activities and be available for a short period every day to answer questions. Most are supported by an in-situ manager who deals with more serious issues. The more you pay for your holiday, the better your rep should be. The best are service-oriented French speakers... but it is difficult to recruit hard-working, intelligent, bilingual people to work for next to nothing. If you want to know what - or who - to expect, ask when you book.

DIY

If you DIY, you have more control over the kind of holiday you take and what you pay. But as you have to make all the arrangements, you'll need more time to plan the trip.

Several **airports** are within transfer distance of Val d'Isère - so you can fly to whichever one has the most convenient flights for you. The major airports are Geneva and Lyon St. Exupéry, which are serviced by the major airlines (BA, Air France or Swiss) as well as some of the budget options (such as Easyjet and bmibaby). Some of the budget airlines also fly to the smaller airports of St. Etienne, Chambéry and Grenoble. The cheapest flights are normally from London, and the earlier you book the

cheaper it will be. The airlines accept reservations for the upcoming winter from around June or July. Some chartered airlines such as Monarch or Thomas Cook may also have a limited number of seats for sale. For **transfers** to Val d'Isère you have a variety of options (➙ getting there). If you don't want to fly, the excellent European motorway system makes **driving** to the Alps surprisingly easy. Getting there by **train** is also an option.

19

On a DIY trip the choice of **accommodation** is endless - you are not restricted by brochures or company deals... however the easiest way to book a chalet or an apartment is through a company or website offering accommodation only, such as Interhome or ifyouski.com. You can liaise with the owners directly if you can find their details, but this is often difficult. For hotels you might be able to get a discount off the published price by contacting them directly. For more information on hotels, chalets and apartments ➙ accommodation.

In **resort** is perhaps where the difference between DIY and package is most noticeable. There is no rep on hand so you have to buy your own lift pass, organise your own equipment rental... but this can have its pluses: you can be sure that you get exactly the right type of pass and you can choose which rental shop you use.

Though the journey is simple enough, Val d'Isère is not close to anywhere and so getting there is always a bit of a slog. The road up from Bourg isn't filled with hairpins like the road to Verbier or La Plagne, but it is a single lane road and is longer than you might think. With snow on the ground the going can be painfully slow.

20

All contact details for the transport listed can be found in the directory.

overland

The most common starting place for any journey by **car** to the Alps is Calais. You can reach Calais from the UK by the **eurotunnel** or **ferry**. Then by car it is just under 1000km to Val d'Isère- a journey that can be done in 11 hours or less. The journey from Calais takes you east of Paris, through Reims to Dijon, then down past Bourg-en-Bresse. Around Lyon you head east towards Moûtiers, then on to Bourg St. Maurice and up to Val d'Isère.

There are 2 *péage* (toll) stops on the route south through France, for which you collect a ticket as you enter the motorway and hand it in as you leave. Expect to pay around €50 in total - you can pay with cash or by credit card.

There are 2 alternatives to the standard **ferry** crossing to Calais. The first is with Norfolkline to Dunkirk - often quieter (and less prone to lorry strikes!) than the Calais services. The second is SpeedFerries.com - a new fast ferry service to Boulogne. SpeedFerries sells tickets on a similar basis to the budget airlines - the earlier you buy, the less you pay.

Eurolines runs **coach** services from the UK to Bourg, from where you can transfer up to Val d'Isère. Once you get to Bourg, there are regular coach services (with Cars Martin) from the train station to the resort.

Travelling by **train** to the Alps gives you more time in resort - 8 days instead of the usual 6 - a particularly excellent service if you live in London. The stop for Val d'Isère is Bourg St. Maurice. All train services from the UK become full months in advance so be sure to book well ahead - tickets are available from the July before the start of the season. The **snowtrain** is the classic way to travel by train to the Alps. You check in at Dover on Friday afternoon, take a ferry to Calais where you board a couchette (a train with sleeping compartments) and travel overnight, arriving in the Alps on Saturday morning. The return service leaves the following Saturday evening.

Another option is the **eurostar overnight** service, which leaves London Waterloo (with some services stopping in Ashford, Kent) on Friday evenings. You travel directly to Paris, where you change onto a couchette to

21

fly-drive p.23

copyright qanuk 2004

travel overnight. As with the snowtrain you arrive in the Alps on Saturday morning and return on Saturday evening. The **eurostar direct** service runs during the daytime, leaving London Waterloo on Saturday mornings and arrives on the Alps on Saturday evenings. The return trip departs on Saturday evening.

22

If you can't get onto the Eurostar services, the French intercity service is an option, a journey that is best started in Paris. The journey to Bourg takes around 4½ hours. To get to Paris, you can either fly or take the Eurostar. The transfer from Bourg is the same as for overland coach travel.

by air

Lyon St. Exupéry (220kms) and Geneva (175kms) are the 2 closest international airports to Val d'Isère - though the greatest number of flights are to Geneva. There are less frequent air services to St. Etienne (300kms), Grenoble (200kms) and Chambéry (145kms).

transfers

The standard transfer time from Geneva or Lyon is 3-3½ hours in a car and with a clear road. Conversely on a coach and with Saturday traffic you'll be lucky to make it in fewer than 4-4½. The journey to Aime takes you through Albertville, which would benefit from a failed Swampy protest and a bypass. The volume of Saturday traffic is

extraordinary - and subject to strict policing throughout the day. Val d'Isère's English tour operators split their transfers between Saturday and Sunday. This keeps the single lane road up from Bourg St. Maurice much less clogged than it otherwise would be (and keeps the town and pistes somewhat quieter on the weekend than during the week). Your choices are a busy Saturday transfer and a quietish Sunday on the piste or an easier transfer on Sunday (but you will miss out on a good day of skiing).

Getting to Val from any of your arrival airports by **car** can be done. You can hire a car at any of them - book over the phone, on the internet, or when you arrive at the airport. Your car will have the necessary equipment such as an emergency triangle, but you will need to specifically ask for snow chains and a roof box if you want them.

From Lyon, Grenoble and Chambéry you can get to Val d'Isère easily by train - there is no direct service from Geneva, which makes it a more tiresome option.

If you don't want to have to worry about driving yourself, there are a number of companies which run **private minibus transfers** from the airport direct to your accommodation. Services vary from a simple pick up and drop off to the provision of welcome packs and food and even champagne during your trip. There are a number of

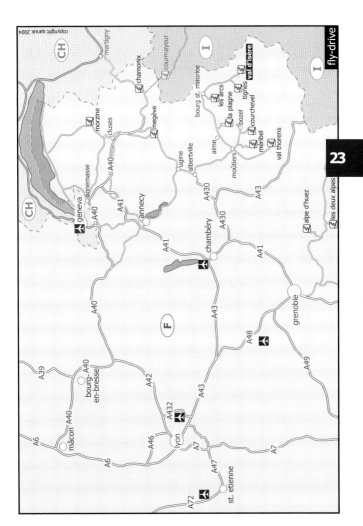

fly-drive

services including ATS, Alp Line, Mountain Transfers and Alpine Cab. All of them take online bookings, either via email or direct through the relevant website. ATS run shuttles from Geneva. Most of Alp Line's services run from Geneva though they will pick up from any of the French airports (though this costs more). Mountain Transfers pick up from Geneva, Chambéry and Lyon St. Exupéry and also Bourg St. Maurice. Alpine Cab is the luxury option, picking up from Geneva, Grenoble, St. Etienne and Lyon. If you don't want to share your personal space with anybody else you can always take a **taxi** - though the privilege of doing so isn't cheap. If you want to get a bird's eye view of the lines of traffic stretching down the route to Val **helicopter** transfers from Geneva, Lyon and Chambéry are possible through SAF Hélicoptères.

24

As you come out of the last in the long line of tunnels up the mountain and into the Isèran valley the first place you reach is La Daille, home to the Funival funicular, a couple of big apartment blocks and a handful of hotels and restaurants. A little further along the same road you get to Val proper, a long thin town which is the HQ for most holidays in this valley. Further along the road you come to Le Laisinant and then Le Fornet, both of which are small communities with a limited range of activities.

You can travel the length of the 4 towns on the *Train Rouge*, Val's free ski **bus** shuttle service. There are in fact 3 different services, but the likelihood is that you'll only take one. The buses - many of which are long concertina style and can carry loads of people - run regularly and the system is as efficient as could be hoped given the large volume of skiers moving around the resort at more or less all times of day. The regular service runs from early enough in the morning to get you to the first lift from wherever you are, and finishes at 7pm. After 7pm there is a sporadic service through until 1:30am.

Val d'Isère is not a big place. There's not much to navigating your way around town - there are basically 2 roads which run parallel to each other, and most of the commerce is on the main drag that leads up to the Front de Neige - the snow front at the bottom of

snapshot

from val by road to
bourg st. maurice 30 minutes
tignes 20 minutes
moûtiers 45 minutes
la plagne 1 hour 20 minutes
st. foy 35 minutes
arc 1800 1 hour
vallandry 1 hour 10 minutes
la rosière 40 minutes

25

the main hub of lifts in the resort. Even the most cartographically challenged person should be able to find their way around. You can walk the length of the town in about 15 minutes in ski boots - assuming you don't stop for a browse in any of the shops or a sneaky vin chaud. Walking into town from La Daille takes about 20 minutes, as does walking south of town out to Le Laisanant. Le Fornet is a bus ride.

At the end of the day on the slopes, you probably won't mind where you rest your head. But when planning your holiday, you might want to put more thought into where you stay.

Tourist beds in Val d'Isère total almost 30,000, and cover the full spectrum of accommodation from the Barmes de l'Ours hotel (Val's only 4* *luxe*) down to the parking lot in La Daille where you can park your camper van for about €10 per night. Self-caterers are well catered for by an abundance of résidences and rental apartments, and there are a lot of traditional chalets available either through the tour operators or as private rentals.

To encourage holidaymakers to book direct, all of Val d'Isère's accommodation (apart from that offered by the tour operators) is now centrally registered on a computer system that allows you to book everything online (i valdisere.com). This system also offers various packages that include a lift pass - and if you book the two at the same time it will all work out a little cheaper. The website is generally very good, though for accommodation searches you will either need broadband or a lot of patience.

hotels

With a range that includes some places you probably can't afford and some where you'll wonder why you're paying so little, Val is not short of diversity in the hotels department. Perhaps surprisingly given its status, there are few hotels in Val d'Isère's that would challenge for a spot on the Alpine podium. However, while they cannot compete with Courchevel 1850 for sheer grandeur or volume, the upper echelon of Val hotels is as impressive as it is small. In fact in general you will find a very high level of service - this is true both of the upmarket and the downmarket options, though nothing can match the flawlessness of the Christiana, the Blizzard and the Barmes de l'Ours.

specifics

Some hotels will only accept week-long **reservations**, especially if you are booking a long time in advance. Outside of low season, last-minute bookings are likely to be relatively difficult to make, though the number of beds in the valley means you are likely to find something somewhere - if you are determined enough to spend a day by the phone. In France the number of **stars** a hotel has is directly connected to its facilities. Things like room size and whether there is a lift dictate how many stars are awarded. Where the rating system can be misleading is in the divide between 2* and 3*. Often a room in a 3* hotel will not be noticeably different to a much cheaper room in a hotel with 1 less star. Nonetheless the 4* hotels are generally the most comfortable and have the widest range of facilities.

26

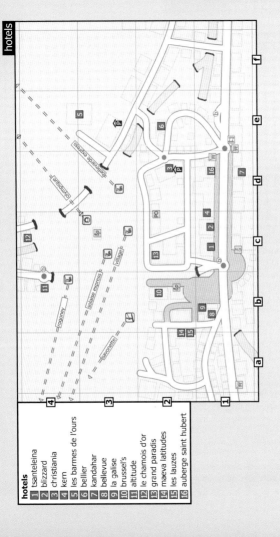

27

Some of the larger hotels - places like the Barmes de l'Ours and the Maeva Latitudes - have their own on-site **rental shop**. Many of the others have a deal with a specific shop in town - they will advise you of this when you check in. If you book your hotel through a tour operator they will almost certainly sort out your rentals for you - and there are also companies who offer a ski-delivery service (➥ skis, boots & boards). There are only a few hotels into which you can actually ski, but broadly speaking when you run out of piste you won't have far to walk to get home, and you're bound to pass a bar or two on the way. Every front-of-house employee will speak **english**, so unless you have a quibble with a cleaning lady you will be able to survive with no French at all. But hotels are where you will notice a difference if you can speak in French. Staff are more likely to be more sympathetic to questions (or complaints) if you make the effort to communicate with them in their language.

28

prices
The price ranges are approximate figures for a double room per night in high season, including tax but not service.
luxury over €150
mid-range €80-150
budget €30-80
All hotels accept most credit cards. Unless otherwise stated, all bedrooms are en-suite (a shower or a bath).

---

snapshot

for...
as cheap as chips - kern
ski in the door - brussel's
peace and quiet - le chamois d'or
luxury - christiania
excess - les barmes de l'ours
good food - blizzard
middle of the action - tsanteleina
best of everything - blizzard

accommodation

<< luxury >>

christiania**

☎ 0479 060825
📞 0479 411110
@ welcome@hotel-christiania.com
W³ hotel-christiania.com
🛏 69 (b&b, ½, full)

p27
d1/2

Val's most refined hotel is charged with professional yet homely atmosphere, displays a consummate and impeccable attention to detail, and has service that could compete with almost any hotel in the Alps. The beautiful red and green décor gives it an intimate and individual feel, and it is a more refined and less showy offering than the Barmes de l'Ours. Location is perfect too - the Front de Neige is a pole's throw away, and in the evenings you can sip a cocktail in the Face while the kids party across the road in Dick's (➜ après-ski & nightlife). Though it lacks the restaurant class of Chamonix's Albert Première and the modern chic of Courchevel's Melezin, the overall package is superb and if you're splashing out on accommodation you could do worse than throw your pennies here.

blizzard**

☎ 0479 060207
📞 0479 060494
@ information@hotelblizzard.com
W³ hotelblizzard.com
🛏 73 (b&b, ½, full)

p27
c1

The very definition of 'chalet style comfort', the Blizzard is what many alpine hotels aspire to be. Spacious and beautiful wood-beamed rooms, 2 excellent restaurants including the Luge (➜ eating out), in-house physio and beauty therapy, an outdoor heated swimming pool... it is wonderful not so much for its homely detail as for the cosy atmosphere it all creates - enough that non-residents make up over two-thirds of the clientele in the comfortable hotel bar. While other places concern themselves with helicopter transfers and fat cigars, the Blizzard sees past the glitz and fur of the 4* luxe and simply offers a genuine welcome and top-end service in surroundings you won't want to leave come hell or high snow levels.

29

les barmes de l'ours**luxe**

☎ 0475 000602
📞 0475 523569
@ welcome@hotel-les-barmes.com
W³ hotel-les-barmes.com
🛏 64 (b&b, ½, full)

p27
e3

Val's first 4* luxe, the Barmes is Val's most expensive hotel by a country mile, and has services and rooms to match its price bracket. Each of the 5 floors has its own decorative theme, rooms range from cosy to giant-sized - and everywhere there are small extravagances: where other hotels have satellite TV, here you get it on a plasma screen; every bath has bubble jets; every room has a balcony;

accommodation

30

family rooms are well partitioned and have 2 separate entrances so you (or the kids) can come and go as you please... it is all organised so attentively you get the feeling that if you dropped your hat, someone would catch it for you. On the skiing side the Barmes works with the ESF (➔ lessons & guiding) and Killy Sport (➔ skis, boots & boards: there is an outlet in the hotel), and there is a free shuttle bus to pick you up from La Daille at the end of the day. With 3 restaurants, live music every night in the bar, a fitness suite, pool, spa, and computer games room, it's difficult to imagine when you'll have time to ski.

<< mid-range >>

brussel's***

☎ 0479 060539
✆ 0479 411669
@ brussel.resa@wanadoo.fr
W³ -
🛏 53 (b&b, ½)

You could literally ski in the door of the Brussel's, and much as with the Grand Paradis its location is very much its selling point. Unlike the Paradis, however, the Brussel's also boasts a beautiful stone-walled restaurant and the smoky and hectic Saloon bar (➔ après-ski & nightlife) - which combine to mean that on some evenings you probably won't have to leave the hotel (before 2am). Though not cramped, the rooms are not huge and the best thing about them is

the view... but though Lynn Truss' panda wouldn't think much of the name, the Brussel's [sic] is a fine hotel which couldn't be better placed.

grand paradis***

☎ 0479 061173
✆ 0479 411113
@ grandparadis@wanadoo.fr
W³ hotelgrandparadis.com
🛏 40 (½, full)

Though a number of Val hotels aren't far from the slopes, the Paradis is one of the few that is properly ski-in ski-out. It is only yards from the Solaise Express and the Olympique cable car and where the ski schools meet; and with a huge terrace on the Front de Neige, if you fancy a day of slope-side sunbathing you simply have to walk out of the front door. Rooms vary by price and quality depending on whether you choose 'traditional' or 'Austrian' style, and whether they face the village or the slopes. It is all somewhat bigger than it is nice, but you can't fault the location.

altitude***

☎ 0479 061255
✆ 0479 411109
@ booking@hotelaltitude.com
W³ hotelaltitude.com
🛏 40 (b&b, ½, full)

Up at the Rond-Point by the Solaise cable car, the Altitude is entirely separate from

Val's bustling streets and bars, and makes for a very different kind of stay. The hotel is in the 3* cosy chalet style, with wooden beams, open fires and fitness rooms, and it is all reasonably priced given the location; but staying at the Altitude is more about staying a little bit away from the action. Chez Paulo and the Gourmandine are just outside the door, but aside from those it's a short walk across the snow if you want to eat or drink or shop. This means there's not a constant stream of noise passing under your balcony, and you can ski-in and ski-out without having to negotiate huge terraces like those of the Grand Paradis and the Brussel's.

for those who want comfortable accommodation and the Espace Killy (the Daille funicular is only just across the road) while keeping the delights of Val at arms length. Rooms are compact but well appointed, there are 2 restaurants and a bar, and though La Daille is hardly the party centre of the Alps, making your way in to Val is only a matter of 20 minutes' walk or a phone call to a taxi company. There is nothing grandiose about the Samovar - it is far more a small and friendly place.

31

le samovar***

☎ 0479 061351
☏ 0479 411108
@ samovar@wanadoo.fr
𝖶³ lesamovar.com
🛏 20 (b&b)

val d'isère

la daille

The only La Daille hotel not run by a tour operator, the Samovar is the choice

kandahar***

p27 d1   7

☎ 0479 060239
☏ 0479 411554
@ hotel.kandahar@netgdi.fr
𝖶³ skifrance.fr/73304/kandahar
🛏 41 (b&b, ½)

A large chalet hotel above the Billabong and Quiksilver shops, the Kandahar is a cosy Savoy style place which boasts as its greatest asset the Taverne d'Alsace restaurant - an excellent place to eat and drink: booth like seating makes for a chatty atmosphere, the menu features traditional Alsacian dishes, and the bar is one of the few places in Val that serves champers in properly chilled glasses. Rooms are more functional than luxurious, and the side-alley entrance isn't quite as impressive as the street-front façades of the Tsanteleina or the Blizzard, but there is little to complain about.

accommodation

maeva latitudes****

☎ 0479 061888
📞 0479 061887
@ latitudes@valdisere.com
𝒲³ valdisere.com/latitudes
🛏 88 (½)

32

Run by the accommodation giant Maeva, the Latitudes hotel is very large and rather lacking in character. Rooms are adequate without being spectacular, facilities are as diverse and complete as you would expect from a 4-star hotel, and the Latitudes boast a very large foyet-cum-piano bar that makes a fine pre-dinner hangout; there is also an in-house massage service, and ski rental shop in the foyet... but there is something processed about the Latitudes that gives it an impersonal feel - justified or excused perhaps by the fact that it is a step (or two) cheaper than its competitors.

tsanteleina***

☎ 0479 061213
📞 0479 411416
@ mattis@hoteltsanteleina.com
𝒲³ hoteltsanteleina.com
🛏 74 (b&b, ½)

About as central as you could hope to be in Val, the Tsanteleina has undergone a number of renovations in its half-century of existence to bring it to its current state of shiny luxury. Rooms come in both chalet and more modern styles, and are

comfy and at the top end very spacious. The hotel has quite a grand feel - and the bar and restaurant are decent and well finished. Outside the doors you can get to almost anywhere within 5 minutes' walk, and while it isn't quite on the level of its next door neighbour the Blizzard, it's a fine choice nonetheless.

<< budget >>

le chamois d'or**

☎ 0479 060044
📞 0479 411658
@ welcome@hotelchamoisdor.com
𝒲³ hotelchamoisdor.com
🛏 24 (b&b, ½)

Up by the Rond-Point, the Chamois d'Or has excellent access to the Espace Killy, and while it is much the same price as the Altitude, it feels more cosy and less ski-resorty than its 3* neighbour. It has some wonderful stone walled rooms, a well-regarded restaurant, quiet surroundings, and though it is the wrong side of the Front de Neige for most of Val's evening activities, the excellent Clochetons restaurant is a shortish walk away.

les lauzes**

☎ 0479 060420
📞 0479 419684
@ lauzes@club-internet.fr
𝒲³ hotel-lauzes.com
🛏 23 (b&b)

A small and very pleasant hotel that dates - as a building at least - from long before the invention of skiing and resorts. Right next to the church in the old Val village, the Lauzes is rather quieter than some places - while still being perfectly close to everything (only 2 minutes from the Front de Neige and the same from the town centre). It is pricey given its lack of luxuries, and there is a supplement for the top floor rooms, but it is still cheaper than places that boast a gym you're never going to use anyway.

kern**

```
p27
c1        4
```

☎ 0479 060606
🖷 0479 062631
@ le-kern@valdisere.com
🕸³ le-kern.valdisere.com
🛏 18 (b&b)

A well-hidden little hotel which feels rather out of place amongst Val's showy splendour. It's pretty basic in every way, and if you stay here you won't be sipping champagne on your balcony gazing at sunset over the mountains... but for the price you can't complain: you could be paying 5 times as much around the corner in the Christiana. It's much like an English b&b - you get a buffet meal breakfast and then you're on your own. This is hardly a problem given how close you are to any number of restaurants and bars - indeed the Kern is perfectly placed for wandering around the middle of town, and if you can fend for yourself the Kern has most of what you need.

paradis-killy?

The world of skiing is changing. You can see it in the marketing of Paradiski's Vanoise Express link, or in the construction of Arc 1950. Chamonix, the resort most likely to make you buy an ice axe, now has a Chanel shop. And Val is changing too - though it is already in the upper echelons of chic, it has always been a little more about snow than show. But with the opening of the 4* *luxe* Barmes de l'Ours the town finds itself in the Courchevel arena of fur coats and designer labels. Somebody somewhere must have noticed that there is money in the Courchevel pastime of going skiing just to hang around the resort and look pretty - and he must have told all his friends. The Barmes applies 21st century finance and design to ski resort culture, and brings Courchevel's philosophy of extravagance to a resort which is more about true skiing than motorway cruising - with a price tag to match. Only time will tell where else the changes reach - but even hobbits with rings would struggle to rid the skiing world of the shift away from a simple love of slopes and snow.

accommodation

chalets

Chalet holidays cater for those who want to stay in a relatively relaxed setting, but don't want to fend for themselves. There are oodles of chalets in Val d'Isère, so you will have plenty of choice about what, where, and how much.

tour companies

All of the major highstreet tour operators run chalet holidays to Val, as well as a number of ski-specific companies and a large number of smaller independently run chalets in and around the town. Staying in a chalet is effectively like staying in someone's house - generally speaking there will be a kitchen, a lounge area, and a number of bedrooms. Chalets come with their own chalet host, who will provide you with breakfast, afternoon tea, and on 6 nights out of 7 an evening meal with wine. As with everything else, the full range is available - some are pretty basic and some are unspeakably luxurious such as the popular Eagle's Nest.

independents

There is a lot of privately run accommodation in the valley - and whereas in places like Chamonix is can be difficult to find, thanks to the Val's central registry system it is not too hard to track down what you want. The internet is also a good place to look - some owners have their own websites or list their chalets on sites such as ifyouski.com. What is on offer in privately run chalets varies greatly. Some provide a similar package to those run by tour companies, some are bed & breakfast only, and in some you are left entirely to your own devices.

résidences

Résidences are effectively large and well appointed apartment blocks. Most have their own gym, bar, swimming pool, sauna and so on - but they are basically self-catering accommodation with a nice foyer. Apartments house between 2 and 8 people, often in 2 or 3 adjoining rooms (some have up to 6) which will be kitted out with full kitchen facilities and bed linen - all you need to bring is some food. There are résidences throughout the town, including the 4* **alpina lodge** (t 0479 41600, i alpina-lodge.com) and 3* **domaines du soleil** (t 0479 062289, i domaines-du-soleil.com) along with sizeable offerings from **maeva** (i maeva.fr) and **pierre & vacences** (i pierreetvacences.com).

apartments

An apartment for 4 is generally 2 rooms (a bedroom and living room), with 2 guests sleeping on a sofabed. On the face of it, they are the cheapest place to stay. But when you add in the price of food and meals out, you can pay more overall than you would pay for a hotel or chalet. However if you can live like a sardine and stay disciplined about what you spend on food, it can be cost-effective. As with chalets, apartments can be found through the tourist office or through agencies in town. Some UK tour operators rent accommodation-only apartments. Prices vary depending upon whether it is high, mid or low season. As a guide, a short-term let for a mid-grade apartment with 2 rooms (4 beds) costs approximately €1000 in high season and €300 in low season. Some apartments are available on a long-let if you want a place for the season. The demand is high so make sure you book early - details of available rentals are kept at the central booking office, Val Location (t 0479 060660, i valdisere.com).

camping

You won't find anywhere to pitch a tent in the winter months, nor is there really a winter caravan site. You can stay in campers or caravans in the large car park in La Daille for a small nightly charge, or out in Le Laisinant for no nightly charge.

a cheaper option

Staying in the centre of town is not cheap - and as a general rule the further out you go, the less you pay. Val's outskirts consist of chalets (which aren't cheap) and apartments (which are cheap - or cheaper, at least). Out of town the average price drops dramatically. Val's 3 satellite towns may not have the range of après options that the main town does, but you can save more than the price of a taxi fare by staying out of the smoke.

la daille is the obvious choice - the nightlife is limited but you can walk into town in 20 minutes or so, and in the morning you have the FuniVal on your doorstep. The only hotel is the Le Samovar (➜ hotels) and most of the accommodation is run by tour operators - though it is still possible to book direct. Pierre et Vacances (t 0479 413030, i pierreetvacences.com) have a typically giant apartment block, and Maeva have a standard 3* residence (t 0479 067676, i maeva.fr). A small number of private rentals are available, including the Maison André (t 0479 060682, i cascade-location.com) and La Vieille Maison (t 0479 060358).

Staying on the other side is also very possible - though **le laisinant** doesn't have a lift, you can ski down to the village and the bus comes past pretty regularly. The 3* Becca (t 0479 060948, i labecca.fr.st) is the only hotel. MGM operate a résidence called Les Chalets du Laisinant (t 0479 066306, i residences-mgm.fr) and private rentals include Les Arcoces (t 0479 060060), La Carline (t 0479 060478) and Chalet Laffont (t 0479 062152). Further out, **le fornet** has a more sizeable community, a cable car up to the skiing, and the lovely L'Aroley restaurant. Accommodation is largely privately owned - details of available rentals are kept at the central booking office, Val Location (t 0479 060660, i valdisere.com).

35

Once you've arrived in Val d'Isère and found where you're staying, there are a few things to do before you can get into the slopes. For many people, long queues and language barriers make this the worst part of the holiday. Starting with lift passes, the following pages take you step by step through the process and how to survive it.

36

There's nothing very complicated about lift passes in the Espace Killy. No electronic tagging, no faffing about with different areas and so on... and single day passes aren't cheap, so you simply need to work out how old you are and then buy a pass for the number of consecutive days you want to be on the slopes. If you plan to take a day off in the middle of the week, you are better off with 2 separate passes instead of paying for a day you don't ski - the by-day reduction isn't so large as to make missing a day cost effective.

the espace killy pass
The pass covers the entire ski area, and is available for anything from half a day to 21 days. You need a photo for passes of 2 days or longer. Should you have the means to get there, a 6 day pass qualifies you for a day's skiing in Paradiski, the 3 Vallées, and Valmorel, and also reduction on passes for La Rosière and St. Foy. A 7 day pass also allows you free access to the swimming pool (➥ activities). The Train Rouge ski bus is free regardless of whether or not you have a pass.

snapshot

useful information
only 1 type of pass available
photo needed for passes of 2 days or more
fidelity reductions for Val d'Isère regulars
there are enough free lifts that beginners may not need to buy a pass

handy to know
There are lift pass offices just below the *Front de Neige* (the snow front) and also by the Solaise Express chair, under the Sun Bar. In La Daille you can buy your pass from the desks by the Funival, and similarly you can buy passes by the cable car in Le Fornet. Remember you will need a passport sized photo for a pass of 2 days or more. All offices open between 8:30am-9am, staying open until mid-afternoon during the week and until the early evening on Saturdays.

With only 1 type of pass available there's nothing very complicated here. The per-day price reduces as the number of days increases, and that's all there is to it. There are **discounts** for **children** (aged 5-12) and **seniors** (aged 60-74) on production of some ID. Children **under 5** and Seniors over **75** ski for free - though you will still need to get a pass. Should you want to you can buy a pass for 14 non-consecutive days throughout the season, but this barely works out cheaper than buying 14 single day passes.

There's no **beginner** specific pass - but if you are a true debutant and are unlikely to leave the Front de Neige, you won't need a pass at all - there are 3 free low-level lifts on the Front de Neige and 1 at La Daille, leaving you with more money to spend on your instructor's lunch.

If you're an Espace Killy **regular**, you can get a small (fidelity) reduction on the price of your pass on production of an old pass. All passes from the previous 3 seasons are accepted (excluding single day passes), and the reduction varies by the week - reductions are larger still in low season. Children's passes also merit this reduction.

Though the Espace Killy in winter doesn't offer much to stimulate the non-skier, **pedestrian** passes are available, either by the day or for 6 days. They are appropriately cheap, and are only valid for 1 return journey in the Val area. If you somehow manage to wind up in Tignes, you'll have to buy another pass to get back.

If you lose your pass or are hurt and can't ski, the only way to get a refund is to have the Carré Neige **insurance** - you can buy it with your pass, bumping up the daily price by a Euro or 3. Without it, you will not get a refund no matter how hard you try. If the weather is bad enough to close every lift for a number of days, a pass of 3 days or longer will be refunded for the number

of days the system is closed, less 1. So if every lift is closed for 3 days of your 6 day pass, you would be refunded for 2 of the days you couldn't ski. Carré Neige also covers you for the cost of search, rescue and ambulance recovery for all skiing accidents on- and off-piste. If you are on a package trip the likelihood is that the package includes ski insurance - but often this does not cover off-piste accidents. It is worth checking when you book.

37

Ski and board hire in Val d'Isère is a choice between quality and economy. The best rental shops have excellent service and equipment, but cost a few shillings more than your average Ski Set. There is a large choice of shops which are all relatively similar, or on the other side of the coin there are a few places which provide assuredly excellent equipment and service but for a little extra monopoly money.

38

handy to know

If you are on a package holiday, the likelihood is that your tour operator will have a deal with a certain store, probably one close to your accommodation. These agreements provide the tour operator with some form of commission and you with slightly cheaper rental - typically 10% off the standard price. Most tour operators use rental shops with staff who are either English or English speaking - though removing the language barrier gives no guarantee of the quality of the service or equipment.

Getting the right equipment will ensure you fully enjoy your holiday. Your feet will hurt if you don't get well-fitting boots so don't be embarrassed to persevere until you find a pair that fits. If they cause you problems on the slopes take them back - all the shops will help you find a more suitable pair. Unless you know you want a specific type or make of ski, take the advice of

the ski fitter. They are the experts and will know which is the best ski for you based on your ability and age.

At most shops you can take out **insurance** (except on test skis) to cover accidental breakage, loss or theft. Skiing on roads is not insurable! Unfortunately skis do get stolen or taken by accident - with so many people having the same makes it's easy to confuse your skis with those belonging to somebody else. When you stop for lunch or après it's a good idea to swap one of your skis with a friend so you both have a mis-matched pair. This helps to ensure that nobody will pick up your skis, either by mistake or otherwise.

for skis

For more than 10 years **precision** have been developing a pro-active and intelligent approach that extends a lot further than simply sticking you in a pair of boots and asking you how much you weigh. Skis and boards are invariably in perfect condition (thanks to SnowTec's Wintersteiger machines), the boot-fitting is internationally respected, the vast majority of staff are native English speakers, and to cap it all they will pick you up from your accommodation and take you to the rental store. For anyone thinking of buying, their La Daille test centre gives you the chance to try the latest equipment on the slopes and with expert advice on hand. Service is exemplary in every department - and while the price may be a little higher than the average, if you're watching your wallet you're in the wrong resort.

Next to the Tourist Office in the centre of town, **killy sport** is the only shop in Val that can rival Precision in terms of service or quality. Though not so pro-active, they stock a similarly impressive range of skis and equipment (though their snowboard section is less well equipped), and offer a similar level of expertise. They deal largely with top-of-the-range equipment and clothing, and between the 2 stores you are likely to be able to find whatever you are looking for: where Precision stocks Salomon and Peak Performance, Killy stocks Arc'Teryx and Patagonia.

ogier is a rising power in ski rental, and as with the Chamonix and Arc 1950 stores the Val branch is a different style of shop to your usual rental place, and is customer-aware in a very different way to Precision or Killy. Much of the clothing on sale has little to do with skiing or mountains, the good quality rental section feels more like a fashion boutique, but the main attraction of Ogier is the fact that it is one of the few places that opens through the frustrating lunchtime siesta.

With 5 shops in Val d'Isère and plenty more in Tignes, **snowfun** is the Woolworths of the Espace Killy. Part of the SnowTec dynasty, this is the clay foot to Precision's golden head. A

decent range of equipment along with quality SnowTec servicing make Snowfun a better choice than many of the random ski houses in the town, and affiliation with the Snowfun ski school means you can wrangle yourself a package discount if you plump for their lessons too.

for boots

Precision can generally cope with anything, but if your problem feet need a more specialist solution, head to **ski mastery**. On the Place du Centre opposite the Tourist Office, they are a small outfit who use postural analysis to identify the right boot for you.

for boards

Renting from a board-specific shop means you will have a decent selection of boards, bindings and boots to choose from, you will be served by staff who know what they're talking about - and if you don't know what you want they will be more likely to pick equipment suited to your level. There are only 2 board-specific shops in Val d'Isère, and aside from Precision's good quality boarding section, you are far better off making the trip to one or the other than settling for sub-standard equipment from a ski shop.

misty fly is one of the best board shops in the Alps. In addition to being well equipped Misty Fly goes some way down the Precision road in terms of service and value. They run a free weekly avalanche awareness course, have their own very experienced snowboard school (→ lessons & guiding), but most significantly have excellent staff and a wide range of boards, accessories and clothing.

hors-piste has an amazingly cramped store that will suit you more than Misty Fly if you're staying on the north side of town. The same principles apply in terms of being served by people who know what they're giving you - but Hors-Piste falls short of Misty Fly because it somehow feels less involved in trying to be helpful and friendly, and also where rentals are concerned, limited size means limited options.

40

for other equipment

Generally rental shops offer a lot more than just skis and boards. From some you can hire touring skis, telemarks, snowblades, snowshoes... in fact more or less anything you might conceivably need or want for the outdoors. The best place to start a search for something in particular is the middle of town. Precision carry everything you can think of, as do Killy Sport - or alternatively Ogier and Jean Sport a little further up will also provide you with specialist equipment like avalanche transceivers, probes and so forth. Val also has its fair share of outdoor (and not-so-outdoor) clothing shops, which also sell various accessories - prices tend to be similar to those in the UK.

ski schools

Ski schools in Val d'Isère are 10 a centime. The ESF (Ecole de Ski Français) exerts a solid presence in the Espace Killy, but it is in strong company - Evolution 2 is very well regarded, and there are a number of smaller schools which offer a more intimate and focussed approach. The general quality of instruction is good across the board - the French qualification requires a very high standard and to teach in France with an English qualification you must be at least BASI 2 qualified. Most English qualified instructors in Val have the BASI 1, which basically means they're very, very good. But qualifications do not a teacher make - as a general rule, the more eggs you employ the more chance you have of getting a rotten one, by which reasoning you are best off with a smaller school, if you're prepared to fork out the extra euros.

specifics

group lessons are the cheapest way to learn to ski. When you book you will be asked your level of skiing/boarding ability, either by the colour of piste you are comfortable on, the number of weeks you have skied before, or by the vague 'beginner/intermediate/advanced' pigeonholes. In practice the divisions aren't as accurate as they could be - some people overestimate their ability or misunderstand words like 'confident' and 'controlled', so to an extent the level of your group is pot luck. If you

41

are honest about your skill level you are likely to find yourself in the right place.

If you have the money, **private lessons** are without question the way forward. Once you're past the basics, individual attention is the best way to significantly improve your technique and is often better value. If you can get a group of 4 or more the individual price per day is similar to the average price per day for group lessons, with the advantage that you go where you want to go and practise what you want to practise. The length of private lessons varies from school to school, but generally the divisions are simply for a half day (morning or afternoon) or a full day. A half day will be 3 hours of instruction on one side of lunch.

42

prices are pretty standard across the board - though you may pay a little more for the smaller companies, there's not much in it. If you book group lessons you can have a week's worth of half-day instruction for only a little more than it costs to rent your skis. Private lessons (and guides) are a different story, but you won't find too much variation in what the different schools charge.

Either make your **booking** before you get to Val d'Isère - by email, fax or phone - or once you're in resort, in person at the ski school office. Always pre-book in peak season, as there are not enough instructors to meet demand - schools recommend booking at least 2 weeks in advance. To confirm your booking, the schools will need your name, level of ability and a credit card number.

The Front de Neige is a hive of **meeting points** - just before 9am every morning the bustle can be rather like walking into a school assembly hall, only outside in the snow. If you book private lessons you ought to be able to choose your own meeting point, and

you would be well advised to choose somewhere other than 'by the Solaise Express'.

It is illegal to teach in France without a qualification recognised by the French establishment. In effect this means that the majority of **instructors** in France are French, as few other 'international' qualifications are accepted and the *equivalence* race test that foreign instructors must pass is extremely difficult. But this approach gives you the advantage of knowing that your instructor is at the least a very competent skier or boarder. Almost all instructors speak good **english** and there are also instructors who speak every other language - though you will need to book a long way in advance should you want instruction in a language less common to the Alps.

Lessons take place **whatever the weather**, unless the entire lift system is closed in which case the school will refund the full lesson price. They will also refund you if you are ill or have an accident and can produce a valid medical certificate. If you cancel a lesson for any other reason, your chances of getting a refund are relative to how much notice you give the school, and how charming you are when you cancel.

esf

☎ 0479 060234
📞 0479 411580
@ esf.valdisere@wanadoo.fr
𝑊³ ski-ecole.com
🖃 chalet esf, village

Despite the number of other ski schools the ESF remains as omnipresent a force as it is everywhere in the French Alps. Its sheer size is its asset and its drawback: the ESF will generally be able to find an instructor who speaks Russian, or Greek, or Swaheli and they have some of the best ski and snowboard instructors in the world - but also some of the worst. The ESF know their stuff, they speak good English. Group classes start with a 'legs back' day on Sunday to assess abilities, then lessons run Mondays-Fridays. Ski levels are officially divided by the colour of the piste you are comfortable skiing on, but in practice function largely as 'beginner', 'intermediate' and 'advanced'. If you are a very proficient skier you are advised to book a private lesson or head to one of the smaller schools.

the development centre

☎ 0615 553156
-
@ info@tdcski.com
𝑊³ tdcski.com
🖃 precision (opp. tourist office)

A small, excellent and exclusively British ski school that operates out of Precision's main store in the town centre. All the instructors are BASI 1 qualified, and instruction is youthful and individual. Along with private lessons, their intelligent approach involves running clinics aimed at developing specific skills rather than simply having you chase a jacket around the pistes. Clinics are run over 2 or 3 half-days, and allow you to choose what you want to concentrate on, either **43** developing skills you already have or focusing on all-terrain skiing, speed and gates or off-piste technique. Given the quality of what you get, they're not expensive, and by the end you're likely to have tried something more challenging than your patience.

oxygène

☎ 0479 419958
📞 0479 419381
@ valdisere@oxygene-ski.com
𝑊³ oxygene-ski.com
🖃 gallerie des cîmes

With a head office in La Plagne it is little surprise that Oxygène is well attuned to teaching children. Though the 10 year-old company is French run, a number of the 20 or so instructors are British. Group sizes are normally kept to 6, and the range of options includes the Tarentaise tour and heliskiing. They are friendly and approachable and will tailor their service to your requirements, and they work with Killy Sport, meaning you can organise your ski rental when you book - which can be done online.

lessons & guiding

evolution 2

☎ 0479 411672
📞 0479 063729
@ valdisere@evolution2.com
W³ evolution2.com
📧 precision (val village)

44

Evo 2 is a lively and young school that is fast becoming recognised as the pretender to the ESF throne. The organisation is more dynamic, more creative, more fashion conscious... in addition to the usual group and private lessons, Evo 2 offers parapenting, ice diving (in the Tignes lake), ski jöering, snowshoeing, helicopter and aeroplane flights, and is the organiser of numerous events throughout the season including the Grand Raid (➤ events & activities). Instruction is generally excellent, and though they lack the intimate and English draw of Mountain Masters or the Development Centre, they are cheaper and in many ways just as good.

mountain masters

☎ 0479 060514
📞 0479 060514
@ info@mountain-masters.com
W³ mountain-masters.com
📧 killy sport

Based downstairs in Killy Sport, Mountain Masters is a small and very experienced ski school. Most instructors are English, and all are very capable teachers. Though they offer group and beginners' lessons,

they specialise in private engagements and top level skiing. Video analysis is a standard feature, and private lessons can be tailored to whatever you fancy. None of it is cheap, but as with most things in the ski industry, you get what you pay for.

BASS

☎ 0679 512405
📞 -
@ valdisere@britishskischool.com
W³ britishskischool.com
📧 -

As the name suggests, the BASS is an entirely English ski school, offering a variety of small-group lessons along with private tuition. The coaching is either general or skill-specific depending on requirement - the specific lessons run on alternate days, giving you the chance to practise a bit in between. Masterclass lessons, open to skiers and snowboarders, include video analysis and a healthy dose of free-ride exploration.

misty fly

☎ 0479 400874
📞 0479 419578
@ lionel.surf@infonie.fr
W³ -
📧 place de l'office de tourisme

Misty Fly is a specialist snowboarding school based in the shop of the same name. The 8 French instructors all speak very good English, and lessons run in the standard group/private fashion, with specialist freeride and freestyle classes during school holidays. They are not expensive, and you can rent your board at the same time as booking your lesson, but the main reason to head here is that you are much better off learning form an out-and-out boarder than from an ESF skier who occasionally dons a plank.

The first ski school to step out of the shadow of the ESF, Top Ski's service is almost exclusively off-piste - based around specialist courses that include heliskiing, touring, steeps and the like. They run pre-season courses from early November, and also an off-piste introduction. Groups are never more than 6 people, and their specialist nature means amongst other things they have a more current knowledge of snow conditions than instructors who have spent the 2 weeks before your lesson teaching kids on the Front de Neige.

and the rest

If none of them whet your appetite there's always posture specialists **ski mastery** (t 0479 401768, i ski-mastery.com), cheap and cheerful **snowfun** (t 0479 419671,

i snowfun.fr), coffee-shop-based **billabong ski & snowboard** (t 0479 060954, i snowboardfrance.com) and the eminently French **valgliss** (t 0479 060072, i valgliss.com).

guides

Though Val d'Isère has a Bureau des Guides (t 0479 069403) in the same way as every ski resort, most of Val's ski schools also employ at least 1 qualified mountain guide. Instructors can teach you how to ski in powder - and the Espace Killy has so much lift accessed off-piste skiing on offer that you can enjoy a powder day without straying too far from the markers. If you want to explore the mountains away from the pistes, the way to do it is to hire a guide. The difference between guides and instructors is fundamental - instructing is about 'how' and guiding is about 'where'. If you like to hike, or want to get away from the crowds, a guide will take you anywhere you are capable of going. On the face of it hiring a guide is expensive (around €300 for a day), but for a group of 4 the cost becomes quite manageable - and if you already know how to ski pretty well, going with a guide is the next step up. Guides will also show you around the pistes - but don't expect them to be too happy about doing it.

45

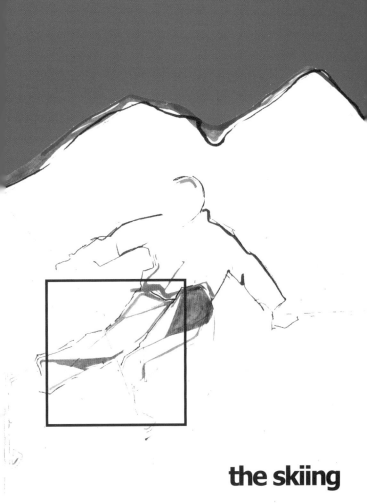

the skiing

The Espace Killy is well known (and well marketed) as one of the finest ski areas on the planet. The 3 Vallées is bigger, Chamonix is more extreme, Zermatt is more beautiful... across the pond Jackson Hole is steeper and Whistler has better snow. But the Espace Killy is the complete package - reliable weather, efficient lifts, pistes for everyone and off-piste for everyone that's good enough or daring enough.

snapshot

vital statistics

300kms of pistes - 22 greens, 69 blues, 34 reds & 15 blacks
99 lifts including 10 free lifts
off-piste - extensive and for all ability levels
highest point - 3450m
longest run - approx 7kms

pistes

48

The Espace Killy has everything - very gentle beginner's slopes, wide and gentle blues, every kind of red, and plenty of challenge in the blacks (though the Tignes side is noticeably steeper). It's all well groomed, and high altitude means good snow on the whole. The most skied and most sunned runs can be a little unpleasant by mid-afternoon - particularly the notorious Face that leads from the Bellevarde back down to the town, as can the runs down to La Daille, which struggle even with artificial cover.

The piste system follows the same colour-coding used in all ski areas throughout Europe (→ 'pistes' in the glossary). You should only use this as a general guide. Although the gradient or width of each individual piste stays the same, other features such as snow conditions can change daily. A blue piste can become more testing than a nearby red, because it is over-crowded with skiers of ranging abilities or because of poor or icy conditions. Personal feelings about pistes vary greatly - an easy blue to one skier can seem like a vertical drop to another. And the general view is that a Val green would be a blue anywhere else and so on up the scale.

off-piste

As much as there is diversity on the pistes, there is also diversity off them. Val has some of the best off-piste runs for beginners anywhere in the Alps, along with which there is a huge amount of lift-accessed powder and some jaw-dropping stuff you will have to hike or skin to get to. Alongside and in between pistes in most areas you will find plenty of ungroomed snow on which to practise your off-piste technique without having to venture too far.

lifts

Val d'Isère has an excellent lift system. There are a lot of new high speed chairlifts, and access to all the areas is very efficient. Relations between the STVI (Val's lift company) and the Val tourist office are not as efficient as they could be, but all you need to worry about is how long you are going to have to queue for and how long it will take you to get to the top of the slopes - and on the whole you are not likely to be disappointed. Peak weeks and peak times can see very long queues, but the speed of the lifts generally means they move pretty fast. There are still a couple of sore thumbs - the unbelievably slow Cugnaï on the Solaise being the most obvious, and the Fornet sector could do with a complete overhaul, but these are minor niggles in an otherwise good system. The story is rather different in Tignes, where the lift company has rather less cash at its disposal and as a result everything is noticeably older and slower.

The glaciers give Val an early start to the season - it is possible to ski in parts of the Espace Killy from November onwards. Specific opening times change from year to year - if you are planning on skiing before you start your advent calendar, contact the tourist office for accurate and up to date information. Most of the lifts open from early December - the remainder being operational by about Christmas.
The exact dates change yearly and if the snow conditions are good, the lifts may open earlier or close later than advertised. During shorter daylight hours in the depths of winter, the lifts close earlier in the day than later in the season when there is light until later. Opening and closing times are noted at

the bottom of some lifts, or alternatively the tourist office will have full details of approximate times for the whole season.

the areas

For the purpose of this guide the Espace Killy area has been divided into 8 sectors which are arranged in sequence from top to bottom (east to west) on the overview map (➜ inside back cover flap) - starting with Le Fornet and ending with Les Brevières. The areas are described further here - those above Tignes are covered in the order you might approach them coming from the Val side of the Espace Killy.

val d'isère
val & la daille (map c)
bellevarde (map d)
solaise (map b)
le fornet (map a)
tignes
tignes & val claret (map e)
grande motte (map f)
tignes west (map g)
les brevières (map h)
In this chapter you'll find a description of how to get to and from the slopes, the general characteristics and aspect of the area, and detail of the pistes, the off-piste, the mountain restaurants and the local après for each area. At the back of the book there is a more detailed table of lift information and a ski map for each area (in which the piste colours correspond to those used by the resort).

49

coming & going

There are 2 main launching points to get you up the hill in the morning. Anyone staying in **val d'isère** itself can walk to the Front de Neige. From there you can get either to the Solaise sector, via the Solaise Express chairlift or the Solaise cable car, or up to the Bellevarde sector via either the Olympique cable car or by combining the Bellevarde Express and Loyes Express chairlifts. Your other option, most useful if you're at the wrong end of town for the Front de Neige, is to catch the bus to La Daille (or to Le Fornet). Coming home is simple too - you either ski your way back down to the Front de Neige (possible from the Solaise and Bellevarde sectors) or just ski down anywhere on the Val side and catch the Train Rouge back into town.

If you're staying in **la daille,** or if for whatever reason you find yourself there on your way to the slopes, any of the lifts is fine. The main route into the Bellevarde sector is the Funival funicular, which comes out in the same place as the Olympique cable car. The gondola and the chairlift take you to the northern edge of the sector, which isn't so convenient for skiing the Bellevarde sector, but which end next to the Tommeuses chairlift, ideal if you're going over to Tignes. You can get back down to La Daille very easily from the Bellevarde sector or from Tignes: it's a straight ski from the Tovière (the

summit that functions as the main crossover point for Tignes, and the top of the Aéroski gondola and the Tufs chairlift). If you're a little further out, you may have to work a bit harder (or think a bit more). The way up from **le fornet** is either on the cable car to the Fornet sector or via the bus to the Front de Neige or La Daille. If you want to ski down you can only do so from the Fornet sector - from anywhere else you'll have to get a bus home. **le laisinant** is worse - there's no lift up, so no matter where you want to go you have to start off on the bus (or it's about a 20 minute walk in to town). Coming home you can ski into Le Laisinant from the Solaise sector. From anywhere else you're on the bus.

beginners

There are a number of free lifts on the Front de Neige - absolute beginners have a huge and gentle snowfield on which to fall over without ever being out of sight of a bar or 4. There is also a small learners' slope in La Daille. The 2 areas above Val d'Isère are both perfect for beginners too. The Solaise has a very open and level area known as the Terrasse, at the top of the Solaise Express chairlift (or the Solaise cable car if you haven't yet mastered chairlifts!). The Bellevarde requires a little more ability, but the 3 greens from the top of the Olympique cable car down to the Marmottes chair offer plenty of easy skiing with a few blues on the side for the more adventurous.

50

intermediates

Much as the Espace Killy is renowned for its excellent off-piste, the domain is perhaps best suited to those who like a cocktail of blues and reds with perhaps just the occasional black thrown in for a bit of spice. It is difficult to recommend one particular area - you can simply go where you please, safe in the knowledge that you will almost always have the choice of something gentle or something steepish.

experts

Lots of the blues in the main areas around Val d'Isère can be skied very fast - but you will have to contend with lots of people travelling much slower than you. The top of the Tommeuses chairlift has a decent mogul run, and is also home to a rut run, but if you're at the top of your game you will find yourself more at home over the ridge in Tignes. The slopes are steeper there, and the bumps are bumpier. The Vallon de la Sache black is the longest bump run in the Espace Killy, and the black from the top of the Col des Vés chairlift features 2 brief but very steep drops. Plus there's the Grande Motte. If your leaning is towards the unpisted side of snow, it matters rather less where you are - after a snowfall you'll find plenty of powder in every sector.

boarders

Much of the Espace Killy is perfect for snowboarding. There are thankfully few very flat runs - a couple of the greens

on the Bellevarde should be avoided, and you will have to hike a bit to avoid the Face on your way home and come down the Santons blue run instead - but on the whole your feet will stay strapped onto your board. This is true of much of the off-piste too - so much of the powder is lift accessed that you will be able to enjoy fresh tracks without having to pull out your snowshoes. One run that is sadly best avoided is the Tour de Charvet (➜ off-piste & touring), which though great fun on skis is basically just a tedious and tiring traverse on a board. There is only 1 proper park (on the Bellevarde), and unsurprisingly 90% of its clientele only take 1 piece of wood with them.

51

summer skiing

The Pissaillas glacier (above Le Fornet) offers enough a handful of blues and reds for anyone who can't survive 9 months without making a turn.

non-skiers

The range of other activities for non-skiers, both on and off the snow, is also extensive, but what there isn't is a lot of walking. Whereas in La Plagne there are in places as many walking paths as there are pistes, in Val there are next to none. You can buy a pedestrian lift pass, but the main reason for doing so is to get to the Signals restaurant (at Le Fornet) for lunch. If you want to explore the mountains on foot, your best bet is to go snowshoeing.

The runs down from the Bellevarde take you to one of 2 places - back down into Val d'Isère, or down to La Daille. Both are home to Olympic ski runs, both are also home to on-mountain après and not a few challenges both on and off the pistes. That said, though they make a good enough destination for leaners and are the only option when coming home from the west side of the Espace Killy, there isn't really enough to warrant spending a lot of time exploring. What you do need to do is make sure of where you're going - though it's easy enough to get from La Daille to Val, heading down the wrong way can leave you half an hour from your power shower.

52

access

From anywhere in Val d'Isère you can walk to the Front de Neige for the Olympique cable car or the Bellevarde Express. The Train Rouge bus will take you to La Daille for the lifts there - or in the other direction if you're based out of town and want to make your way in.

pistes

The **green** run which leads down to La Daille is allegedly the bottom half of the longest run in the Espace Killy. In practice it can be a little difficult to follow, and at times you'll find yourself on the same stretch of snow as plenty of people who think they're on a red.

The notable **blue** is the Santons run, which leads from the bottom of the

map c

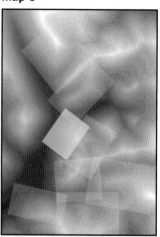

snapshot

out of interest
highest point - 2662m
aspect - e
pistes - a gentle green, a couple of blues, a handful of reds & the face black
off-piste - limited
restaurants - 3

highlights & hotspots
the face
the santons blue can be very busy - and the end is flat
the great shuss down to la daille

Fontaine Froide chairlift down towards the Front de Neige in Val d'Isère. It isn't notable for being fun, however - it is narrow at the top, and flat at the bottom, which leads to collisions on the way down and then walking before you can get to your vin chaud. But if you don't like black, you don't have any other options.

The majority of the mish-mash of pistes leading down to La Daille is labelled **red**. It is all pretty standard stuff, though you will also find the women's Olympic downhill run - which tends to be cordoned off. If you head left over the bridge just down from the bottom of the Solaise chair you come to the least skied of all the runs down - the Trifollet, which runs parallel to the others but which you can't get to (or get off) apart from at the top. This is also the way to the superb little forest track mentioned below in off-piste.

Two **blacks** here - one of which is the men's Olympic downhill run, the Face. It gets a lot of hype - 'skiing the Face' is one of those things everyone talks about after a holiday in Val - but in practice the majority of skiers aren't quite at the required level and so there tends to be a lot of traffic and a lot of side-slipping. Amongst other things this makes the snow uneven, so conditions can be difficult even if you are comfortable with the gradient... the main problem is that it is the main route down to Val d'Isère, so people ski it out

of necessity as much as out of desire. The other black is the Epaule du Charvet, a sideline option from the bottom of the Fontaine Froide chairlift. It's easy to miss the start and wind up on the narrow blue, and the bottom section is flat enough to have everyone poling or walking, but for a short while the drop is steep and there tends to be a fraction of the traffic found on the other 2 options.

off-piste

53

While it is possible to ski down to La Daille from the Summit of the Rocher de Bellevarde, you should not attempt to unless you are very competent and with someone who knows where they're going. Much of the wooded area between the pistes is skiable, and if you come from the Bellevarde sector and hold your altitude to the south of the pistes, you can ski all the way down through the trees - though you need to be careful about picking you route, as there are exposed rocks and some steep drops, the more so the further round the face you go.

From the top of the Trifollet red run you can leave the piste to the left and traverse along through the trees before dropping down to rejoin the marked area - though not long, the trees are well spaced out, making this a good spot to practice.

Alternatively, there is a very narrow track that leads through the bottom of the canyon on the right of the Trifollet run. Appropriately named the Vallée Perdue (the lost valley), it is not too well known nor does it look very appealing, so it's rarely busy. You won't find powder there, but if it's clear it makes an exhilarating way to head down - though it is often very rocky - so don't use it to try out your new pair of Zags.

eating & drinking

54

la tanière (t 0479 061129) is a lovely little restaurant at the top of the Bellevarde Express that opens at 9am for breakfast in the sunshine. If you've made it up before the crowds it can be very satisfying to watch the bustle down on the Front de Neige while you sip your coffee on the terrace... through the rest of the day the restaurant serves a decent menu that is cheaper than some places on the hill and which includes fondue if you order the day before. There is a small upstairs section if you want some privacy, and refreshingly, customers don't have to pay to use the toilets.

The **trifollet** (t 0479 419699) has a small eating section and a menu of snacks and simple dishes (including pizza) - but it is far more bar than restaurant, and has music and volume to match. It is the inverse of the Folie Douce, in that it's quite small and personal and doesn't get much sunshine; the vin chaud is amongst the most expensive in the Espace Killy, but

comes with the benefit of being close enough to La Daille that when you leave all you need to do is point down the mountain and not fall over.

getting home

The slopes end either at the Front de Neige in Val or over in La Daille - so getting back to your accommodation (or getting to a bar) is a matter of walking or catching a bus.

The Bellevarde is a large and relatively gentle area, with a selection of wide green and blue pistes. It could be considered the 'main' ski area of the Espace Killy (on the Val d'Isère side), with 3 mountain restaurants, the Val snowpark, and access to Tignes via the Borsat express and Tommeuses chairlifts. It is also home to some excellent off-piste, including the Tour du Charvet (➥ off-piste & touring), but for the most part the skiing is pretty pedestrian and won't excite anyone looking for adventure: there is little on-piste to push the advanced skier, and unless there's been a fresh snowfall the easily accessed off-piste is likely to be tracked. With pistes in all directions the Bellevarde's popularity is amongst other things due to the fact that it catches the sun all through the day.

access

From Val take the Olympique cable car or the Bellevarde Express followed by the Loyes Express (which is sometimes closed in bad weather). The cable car route is almost always quicker regardless of queues, but those with low tolerance for standing around should take the 2 chairs. From La Daille take the Funival. Taking the Daille gondola or the Etroits chair only gets you to the bottom edge of the area, though this is the quickest way to the Tommeuses chairlift.

pistes

There are a lot of **green** runs - 2

map d

55

snapshot

out of interest
highest point - 2760m
aspect - all directions
pistes - lots of green, some fun blue, a little red & some black runs to get home
off-piste - everything from the Grand Pré chair, the Tommeuses chair & plenty off the sides of the pistes
restaurants - 5

highlights & hotspots
la folie douce and la fruitère
a few flat spots
everything from the grand pré chair
the snowpark

leading down from the Rocher de Bellevarde are pretty flat, as is a stretch of the Borsat piste from the top of the Borsat Express chairlift. The best of the bunch is the run from the Grand Pré, which is wide and never so level that you have to resort to poling.

The 2 best **blues** are the long sweeping run under the Tommeuses chairlift, and the '3J' piste from the top of the Bellevarde down to the Marmottes restaurant, which must be pushing the gradient boundary to qualify it as a red.

The short bump run from the Tommeuses chairlift is **red**, but for a red piste you need the 'Orange', bizarrely, which runs from the Rocher de Bellevarde all the way down to La Daille.

The 2 **black** runs in the sector end up down in Val - this is the launch point for the Face, and for the Epaule du Charvet.

snowpark

The Val snowpark is pretty standard - and rather small if you're used to places like Morzine or the Moon park in Méribel. It opens with a short boardercross course, followed by a line of 3 decent sized kickers with a gentler line off to the side for beginners, and a line of pretty high-level rails. By halfway through the season, and in time for the Big Day Out (➥ events & activitites),

there will also be some rather more serious jumps for proper Big Air practice. The lines are colour coded green, red and black - though the overwhelming majority of those in the park take the red line. The tacit queuing system of most parks is more obvious here thanks to the high volume of people - but as with anywhere else it still consists of waiting around until you reckon it's roughly your turn before heading off.

off-piste

The variety of off-piste is excellent. The lift system provides such good access that on a powder day you are guaranteed fresh tracks without having to hike anywhere - though the fresh snow won't last the day. Anyone who likes walking will be happy, and the Bellevarde is home to the Tour du Charvet and the Pisteur's Couloir (➥ off-piste & touring), but there is also enormous opportunity to nip off the side of pistes or to head back down under lifts - most notably the Tommeuses and the Grand Pré.

eating & drinking

bellevarde (t 0479 060576) is a standard form establishment with a table-service restaurant on the upstairs level and a self-service and snack bar section underneath. Because of its location - just underneath the main entry point to the area, at the top of the Olympique cable car and the Funival - it is always pretty busy. The restaurant has a decent range of food, and between there, the self-service section and the snack bar you can pretty much find whatever you want to suit your stomach, your budget or your timetable.

la folie douce (t 0479 060717) is one of the best known altitude restaurants in the Alps, though its renown is due to noise and atmosphere rather than to quality food. As regards eating, it's a spacious self-service place with a large sun-trap terrace. Over lunchtime, the Folie Douce is an unremarkable self-service restaurant at the top of the Daille gondola. If you're looking for a good meal you are much better off next door at the Fruitière - but on sunny afternoons, the sizeable terrace becomes something of an open air après bar. With live musicians, DJs, and a sound system that could probably start an avalanche or two, the Douce creates an atmosphere to rival any of the bars in town, and is an excellent argument to make an early start on the party part of your day.

Though by no means a gastronomic restaurant, **la fruitière** (t 0479 060717) is one of the best in the Espace Killy. Excellent food, beautifully rustic and colour-coordinated décor (which is all authentic), quality service and not-outrageous prices make the overall package hard to beat. They only serve French produce, only Savoyarde cheese, and the dishes are all heartily sized. If you sit out on the terrace they have hilarious sleeping bag outfits to keep you warm as you eat... and it's joined to the Folie Douce so once you've finished eating you don't even have to go outside before you start drinking.

marmottes (t 0479 060508) is a simple self-service restaurant, with a sometimes-open snack bar for those just wanting a quick stop. At the meeting point of a variety of pistes it is a heavily populated place, and the interior can get very cosy when the weather's not great. Food is standard self-service fare, steak, spaghetti and sausages.

At the crossover point between the Val and Tignes sides of the Espace Killy, **la tovière** is an example of Isèran arrogance. Its location guarantees it good business, and its terrace has a fine view, but the service and prices do not match the food. It is by no means a bad restaurant, but there are many others that make more of an effort and charge you less for the privilege (and the toilets).

getting home

Skiing down takes you into the Val and La Daille sector, bringing you out either at the Front de Neige or in La Daille. If you would rather have a rest you can take the Olympique cable car back into Val d'Isère, or you can catch the Funival or the Daille gondola to head back to La Daille.

An area with something for everyone, the Solaise has flat pistes and steep ones, quick lifts and slow ones, open powder and trees, a couple of good lunch options, and a link to Le Fornet. This all makes it a popular place, so you're not likely to find much peace and quiet. It is a favourite area of many of the ski schools, and you may find more than your share of food queues, but the diversity of attractions are more than enough to compensate. The only downside is the lack of a connecting lift at a high altitude to the Bellevarde sector - if you commit to a day on the Solaise and then decide to venture over to Bellevarde, the only option is to return to the Front de Neige and take the lifts from there.

58

access

There are 2 options from the Front de Neige - either the Solaise Express chair or the Solaise cable car. Unless you're staying up by the Rond-Point, the chair is easier to get to and it just as quick as the cable car - though mid-mornings during school holidays the chair can have an impressive queue and it might be worth making the walk.

pistes

There's a simple and satisfying **green** run from the Madeleine chair, and for absolute beginners the wide open area at the top of the Solaise Express and the Solaise cable car is green and very level.

map b

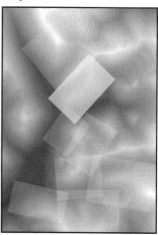

snapshot

out of interest
highest point - 2850m
aspect - n & w
pistes - enough green for beginners, enough blue for everyone, a little red for practice & no black
off-piste - extensive if you know where you're going
restaurants - 3

highlights & hotspots
the cugnaï off-piste run
the cugnaï chair is very slow
the off-piste red down to the manchet chair

Lots of chilled **blue** runs - particularly over by the Glacier Express chairlift - though none of it is simply cruising, as the undulating terrain means your speed is constantly changing.

The 2 main **reds** are the winding run down to the Manchet chair, and the stepp-then-flat run leading back from the Cugnaï chair.

And there is no **black**.

off-piste

The stretch down to the Manchet chair is one of the best 'easy' off-piste options in the Espace Killy. Aside from that there is the Cugnaï valley (if you can survive the painfully slow lift), a tree-level ski called the 'Super L' from the Mattis piste down through the trees, and plenty of space in between the marked runs. It is also possible to ski down from the Terrasse (the top of the Solaise chair and cable car) to the Clochetons restaurant.

eating & drinking

From chips and cheese to beef carpaccio, **la datcha** (t 0479 062114) can cope with most dietary requirements. There's nothing special about the building, but service and food are equally good, portions are large, there's a sizeable sundeck and a self-service section, and if you eat too much to ski anywhere the rope tow back to the Lac lift is just a few yards away.

Basically a glorified snack bar, **l'ouilette** (t 0479 419474) serves a cheapish range of self-service snacks for consumption on the terrace. The plat du jour is as close as it gets to restaurant food - but if you just want somewhere to eat quiche in the sunshine, l'Ouliette is as good as anywhere.

getting home

From the Terrasse there are plenty of routes down to the Front de Neige. Alternatively you can head down to Le Laisinant via the long fast blue from the bottom of the Datcha chair - from there you can catch the bus back to town. Unless you plan to drop off into the Super L (➜ off-piste & touring) there's little reason to ski home down the Mattis red, as it's little more than a track and lower down can be bumpy and icy in poor snow. If you don't fancy the bus from Le Laisinant, there is a track that leads round from the 'L' piste to the Front de Neige - but blink and you'll miss the turn. And it's flat, so boarders are better off taking the bus. To give your legs a rest and get home by lift, work your way to the top of the Solaise cable car - that will take you down into the centre of Val.

le fornet

The south-eastern extent of the Espace Killy is home to the full spectrum of pistes (just), some lesser known off-piste, a superb restaurant, and Val's summer skiing. Le Fornet tends to be less busy than the rest of the ski area - maybe because it isn't so readily accessible, and maybe because it is often pretty chilly (though it is more sheltered than the Grande Motte). There aren't a lot of pistes, and it isn't a great place to learn or somewhere to go if you don't like drag lifts, but if you can cope with its dated access it has much to offer.

60

access

Either take the Train Rouge to the base station, or head up the Solaise first and then take the Glacier Express and Leissières chairs.

pistes

There is a **green** up on the glacier, but if this is the only colour you are looking for you are better off elsewhere.

Most of the Fornet area is blue, and it's pretty solidly inoffensive stuff. You can cruise on a **blue** all the way from the shadow of the Pointe du Montet (at the top of the glacier) down to the Signals restaurant, and indeed on down to Le Fornet.

The Signals drag leads to a refreshingly steep **red** and there are also red options on the glacier.

map a

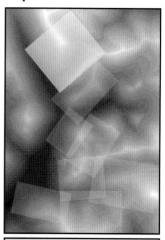

snapshot

out of interest
highest point - 3260m
aspect - n & w
pistes - a little green, a lot of blue & 1 or 2 decent reds
off-piste - extensive and open
restaurants - 4

highlights & hotspots
good snow on the glacier
the rollercoaster Leissières Express
link to the Solaise sector
long blues to cruise on

Like the Solaise Le Fornet has no **black** runs, but the off-piste more than compensates.

off-piste

Much of the attraction of Le Fornet is its off-piste - the Signals drag leads to plenty of very open terrain and the ski down to the base-station cable car can be done through the trees. Much of the terrain that forms the summer skiing area can be skied too - if you're wondering what the purpose of the Pays Desert draglift is, it is the return lift from a number of off-piste runs.

eating & drinking

Arguably the best altitude restaurant in the Espace Killy, **le signal** (t 0479 060338) is the epitome of what the French would call *chaleur* - warmth, both in terms of cosiness and friendliness. An open fire, beautiful decoration, excellent service and a menu featuring delicacies such as oyster and frogs legs along with more regular dishes... if you only eat in one mountain restaurant during your stay, this should be it - and you should reserve your table before you go. For those who don't have the time to savour the Signal's delights, there is also a self-service restaurant downstairs and a take-away oyster joint outside. Being at the top of the Fornet cable car, it is accessible for non-skiers.

A very pleasant and little known restaurant on the Magnard piste (blue) down to the base station, the **edelweiss** (t 0610 287064) has a warm interior and a small terrace that doesn't see too much sunshine. It suffers from being in between Le Signal and L'Arolay restaurants, but if you somehow manage to ski past one and can't manage the walk to the other, the Edelweiss provides a secluded food spot with a proper restaurant menu and an inexpensive 3 course option.

les crozets is not so much a restaurant as a snack bar at the base of the cable car. There's some seating, and if it's seems like too much time and effort to head down to L'Arolay then you can get simple food here and eat it in the cable car on the way back up. Or on the bus on the way back to town.

A short walk from the bottom of the pistes, **l'arolay** (t 0479 061169) is an excellent restaurant that offers plat du jour style lunches in a warm and friendly atmosphere - or on the large terrace on sunny days.

The bottom of the Pays Desert draglift is an excellent spot to break out the tinfoil-wrapped baguettes for a **picnic** - it is a little used lift, and is therefore quiet, and has great views of the Fornet area as well as being the end of a couple of off-piste runs that make good viewing as you munch your jambon fromage.

61

getting home

The runs down to the base station are blue and black - the Forêt run (black) is often officially closed and snow conditions can get pretty unpleasant if it hasn't snowed for a while. The Magnard (blue) is the safer and gentler option. From the bottom, the Train Rouge takes you back to town. Alternatively you can take the Leissières chair to the Solaise area and then ski your way back to the Front de Neige. For a less active option, the Vallon de l'Isèran gondola and the Fornet cable car mean that you can get down to the valley floor from pretty much anywhere without having to ski at all.

62

The area linking Val to its partner in crime has blues, reds, blacks, bumps, some very dangerous off-piste, and leads you either to Val Claret and the Grande Motte funicular or to Tignes le Lac, Le Lavachet and the lesser known western end of the Espace Killy. Coming down from La Tovière the view across the valley is pretty spectacular, and though the area is basically just a way to get to somewhere else, it has plenty of quality skiing in its own right.

access

From the Val side 2 chairlifts - the Tommeuses and the Borsat Express - lead over to the skiing above Tignes. The Borsat only accesses an unchallenging ski down to Val Claret, but it is quieter than the Tommeuses, which leads to the summit of La Tovière and the full range of options.

pistes

Tignes, on the whole, is too steep for **green**, and there is none on the way over from Val.

There is plenty of **blue**, however, including a long and wide and fast descent all the way down to Val Claret.

There is not much in the way of **red**, the middle section of the ski down to Tignes la Lac is red but it is blue at the top and it soon becomes black.

A fine and bumpy **black** leads off to the left from just below La Tovière, and the

map e

63

snapshot

out of interest
highest point - 2695m
aspect - w
pistes - some fast blue, not much red & 2 black options - 1 bumpy, 1 icy
off-piste - limited & mostly very steep
restaurants - 2

highlights & hotspots
limited skiing for true intermediates
access to tignes
little off-piste for mortals
the ski down to tignes le lac is black

ski down into Tignes le Lac is also black - unavoidably so, in fact, and the final schuss can also be very icy (especially in the morning).

off-piste
Most of the area leading down to Tignes is pisted - with the exception of the Tufs, an extraordinary array of narrow couloirs that lead down towards the Lac de Tignes, the lake that separates Val Claret and Tignes le Lac. These are for extremely good skiers only.

64

eating & drinking
You have any number of options in Val Claret or Tignes le Lac themselves. For lunch with a view **la tovière** (➥ bellevarde) is the high altitude choice, or lower down try the restaurant just above Val Claret, at the top of the Bollins chairlift.

getting home
There are lifts from all of Val Claret, Tignes le Lac and Le Lavachet that get you back up and over to the Val side of things. From Val Claret the Tufs and Fresse chairs take you back over to the Val side - from either you can ski all the way down to La Daille or make your way across the Bellevarde sector to ski down to Val itself. The Tufs is a more direct route towards La Daille. From Tignes le Lac the Aeroski gondola takes you to the summit of La Tovière and back into the Bellevarde area, as with the Tufs chairlift. The quickest way back

from Le Lavachet is the Paquis chair, from where you make a short traverse and then take the Combe Folle drag. This leaves you heading down to La Daille - if you want to ski into Val you still have to take the Mont Blanc and then either Marmottes or Borsat Express chairs.

The only way back to Val without skiing is by taxi.

Far above Val Claret on the Tignes side of the ski area, the Grande Motte has the highest skiing in the Espace Killy, and in theory the most reliable snow. In practice it's often very very cold, and can be windy even when the rest of the ski area is relatively calm. It can also have zero visibility when the rest of the area is in sunshine - or conversely can be sunny when the valleys are deep in the clouds. The pisted area is relatively limited, but with a long vertical drop and an array of off-piste options there is plenty to make it worth the trip over.

access

It's quite a way from Val d'Isère to the top of the Grande Motte. It takes a skier of average speed the best part of an hour if there are few queues, and up to two if there's a lot of on-piste traffic. From the Front de Neige, take the Olympique cable car and ski down to either the Borsat Express or the Tommeuses chairlifts, then down to Val Claret. From La Daille any of the base station lifts will get you to the Tommeuses chair. Once you get to Val Claret you can head up either on the Funicular or the Lanches chair. The Funicular is the warmer of the 2 options, but irritatingly it only gets you to the bottom of the Grande Motte cable car, which makes it hardly worth the wait given that you then have to queue again to get to the glacier.

pistes

No **greens** to speak of, but if you head

map f

65

snapshot

out of interest
highest point - 3409m
aspect - ne & e
pistes - no green, some flat but quiet blue, 2 superb reds & 1 fun black
off-piste - extensive, glaciated & needs a guide
restaurants - 2

highlights & hotspots
the run from the top of the cable car is superb
the run from the top of the cable car takes ages to get to

right as you ski down from the top of the Funicular or the top of the Lanches chair, you can enjoy the area's **blue** run - a gentle and peaceful descent all the way back down to Val Claret. A good choice for young children and tentative skiers, the runs are flat in places and though you may have pole yourself along a bit, high speeds are hard to come by so you won't have to worry about getting knocked over.

66

From the top of the cable car, the long and sweeping **red** run across the glacier is a great place to pick up speed and put in some proper carved turns. It is a wide and sustained slope, and the slow cable car service means it is rarely too busy. The ski down to Val Claret under the Lanches chair is often much busier but is a similarly wide and fast descent, which is also home to the Tignes Snowpark.

The only **black** run leads down to the Leisse chair, and is a fun if rather short drop which can be pretty bumpy and pretty busy.

off-piste

This is largely the reason to go to the Grande Motte area - from the top of the cable car there are any number of opportunities for skiing a variety of different ugroomed terrains. Much of this involves knowing where you want to go, and to get the best out of the area you should go with a guide or read up beforehand - the best descriptions

are in the Val d'Isère Off-Piste book by Jean-Luc Steiger & Guy Bonnevie, available from bookshops in the resort.

summer skiing

Much of the summertime glacier skiing is left unpisted in the winter. While the summer runs are often open for a short period in early season, from January onwards the Rosolin, Champany, Double Plan and 3500 lifts are dormant, and their runs are left out of the pisted network. There is also a high-altitude park - down towards the Rosolin drag lifts, but as with the pistes this will only be open for the very start of the winter season.

snowpark

The Tignes park is in many ways very frustrating: it has no service lift, and for much of the season it is ungroomed. Once it does get going, normally mid-February or later, it offers a limited selection of simple rails and small kickers. Consequently it is always quieter than the Val park, so if you don't mind hiking back up (or making the 15 minute round trip on the Lanches chair), it does make a decent place to practice.

eating & drinking

le panoramic is a very large place with spectacular views from the terrace and a lovely indoor table-service section. Food from the self-service area is pretty standard, though the inside is large enough that you'll probably find somewhere to sit no matter how busy it is - and the proper restaurant is separate and beautifully decorated with a warming wood fire. For instant satisfaction, there is a waffle stand outside.

getting home

From the top of the Grande Motte it takes at least an hour to get back to Val - skiing at an average speed - and at the end of the day there are likely to be big queues for the Fresse and the Tufs lifts, so your return time can be significantly increased. Either lift puts you back in the Bellevarde area, from where you can ski down to La Daille or take the Marmottes lift to ski back into Val d'Isère. You can't "lift it" all the way back - you can take the funicular down to Val Claret, but from there you'll have to do some skiing to make it back to Val d'Isère, or take a taxi.

The slopes on the west side of Tignes range from broad and blue to steep and black. The lifts on this side of the valley are noticeably older and slower than the rest of the Espace Killy - but the skiing is as good if not better than in any other area, and the pistes are generally quieter than in the main sectors on the Val side. There's not much in the way of lift-accessed off-piste, nor will you find too many moguls (unless you head over towards Les Brevières) - but there is plenty of range as pisted skiing goes.

68

access
Taking the Olympique cable car from the Front de Neige and then the Tommeuses chair, you can be in Tignes le Lac or Val Claret in under 30 minutes - Tignes Le Lac for the northern end of the sector, on the Palafour chairlift, and Val Claret for the southern, from where you take the Tichot chiar or the Balmes drag.

pistes
Again no **greens**, but most of the area is wide and **blue** - from the top of the Signal, Grattalu or Grand Huit lifts you can ski a gentle gradient all the way down to Val Claret or le Lac. These are great runs on which to practice your technique, or to nip off the side of the piste for a bit of powder training.

There's not a lot of **red** - the slalom run down to Val Claret is often cordoned off, which leaves the short run from the

map g

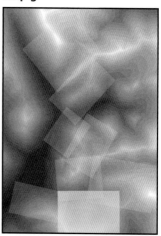

snapshot

out of interest
highest point - 2820m
aspect - ne & e
pistes - no green, a network of blues, a couple of reds & a couple of fun blacks
off-piste - some, though the best is only for the experts
restaurants - 2

highlights & hotspots
the long blue from the Col du Palet drag lift all the way down to Val Claret
the steep sections of the black from the col des ves chairlift

Grand Huit chair and the steep-ish run from the Aiguille Percée chair.

The **blacks** are fun - the most interesting is the run from the Aiguille Percée chair, which you effectively have to hike to get to. It starts with a great rock formation, and the run itself is steep and unrelenting.

off-piste

There is little in the area that can be reached without a hike - though the entire face below the bottom of the merle blanc chair can be skied down to Val Claret, Tignes le Lac or the road joining the two. There a number of couloirs that can be reached from the top of the Merle Blanc, along with the bowl west of the Grand Huit chair - but these involve hiking and are only for strong skiers.

eating & drinking

le palet is in a large and unattractive building, made aesthetically worse by its proximity to the hangar by the Col des Ves chair. Even the terrace is metal and ugly - but it is also very spacious, in addition to which the self-service food is a good as anywhere else and le Palet is far enough from Val d'Isère that you don't have to pay for the toilets.

With superb views of les Tufs and up the valley to Val Claret, **la savouna** is a fine spot if you want to sunbathe with your sandwich. The food is standard snacks and plat du jour - though in the

evening they offer a full-blown Savoyarde menu, after which you can slide back down to town in a bin-bag... though of course if you're staying in Val d'Isère you're the wrong side of a number of mountains.

getting home

From Val Claret take either the Tufs or Fresse chairs or from Tignes le Lac take the Aéroski gondola. These put you back in the Bellevarde area, from where you can ski down to La Daille or take the Marmottes chair to head straight back to Val d'Isère. If you don't want to ski only way back to Val is by taxi.

69

The northern extent of the Espace Killy is home to its lowest skiable point, its longest bumpy black run, and its oldest and slowest lifts. The area below the tree line provides decent bad weather skiing - but if you're staying in Val you'll have a hard time getting to it. Aside from the bumps there is little to advertise the area, except for it being 'somewhere to go', and having in the town of les Brevières enough decent restaurants to celebrate having gone there.

70

access

Take the Tommeuses chair from the Bellevarde area, and ski down towards Tignes le Lac. Stay as far right as you can and head down to le Lavachet, from where you can take the Chaudannes chair.

pistes

There is no **green** in the Les Brevières sector.

You can ski **blue** all the way from the top of the Marais chair to Les Brevières village. Part of the top of the run is flat, but otherwise it is a pleasing cruise. Lower down there are also a couple of other blue options.

The best of the **reds** on offer is the Myosotis run down under the Aiguille Rouge chairlift, which is quite short but is one of those reds that make you feel very satisfied when you get to the bottom.

map h

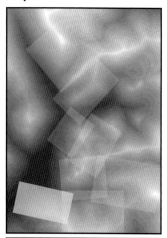

snapshot

out of interest
highest point - 2758m
aspect - n & e
pistes - no green, some cruisey blue, a little red & a lot of black
off-piste - limited
restaurants - 1

highlights & hotspots
the sache black run
the very slow marais chair
some nice restaurants in les brevières
it takes a long time to get back to Val

But the real reason to come to Les Brevières is the **black**. There's a fun bump run under the Marais chairlift, and then there's the Sache. Running the length of the Vallon de la Sache, it is tough, bumpy, exhausting, and you can't opt out once you've started. It takes you right down to Les Brevières - where you can stop and have some chocolate and rest your legs while you try to figure out how far you are from a hot bath and bed.

off-piste
The best of the unpisted area is so skiable that it is marked, and unless there fresh snow it will be very bumpy. The Vallon de la Sache, rated balck, would be marked as an itinerary route in many resorts. If you're looking for powder it is mostly of the side-of-the piste variety, unless you know where you're hiking to.

eating & drinking
l'alpage at the top of the Chaudannes chair is a pleasant offering with both self- and table-service options both inside and out on the terrace. Food is uncomplicated and not too expensive, and the view up the valley is pretty impressive. And it's out of the way enough that it doesn't get as busy as some more central locations.

getting home
Skiing down you can go straight into Tignes le Lac, from where the Aéroski lift takes you up to the Tovière. From Le

Lavachet take the Paquis chair and then the Combe Folle drag. You can then ski down to La Daille, or make your way across the Bellevarde area to ski back into Val d'Isère. As with all other areas in Tignes, if you plan on getting back to Val without skiing, or you miss the last lift, you'll have to return by taxi.

So many pistes, so little time. Often it's difficult to know where to start, where to find the longest runs, or where to go when there's not much snow or the weather is bad. Here are a few suggestions.

top to top glacier race

Though it involves more time on lifts than on pistes, a fun way to nip across the area is to race from the highest lift accessed point on the Grand Pissaillas glacier in Le Fornet to the top of the Grand Motte. It can be done on- or off-piste and you can pick your route, though remember if you're on-piste that you will be passing plenty of people who aren't racing! Top to top should take you less than 2 hours - after which you can race your way back again.

legs back

Though the Bellevarde, Solaise and Fornet sectors are closer if you suddenly get tired, for a first-day look at the Espace Killy that can be done all on blue runs - and with a decent lunch stop - ski a clockwise loop round to Les Brevières. From the Bellevarde area take either the Borsat Express or the Tommeuses and then ski down to Val Claret. Take the Tichot chair up into Tignes West and work your way north and then down to Le Lavachet (the direct ski down to Le Lavachet from the top of the Tommeuses is on a black). From there take the Chaudannes chair and head

down to Les Brevières for lunch. Allow yourself at least an hour to get back to La Daille, and nearer two if you want to ski back into Val d'Isère.

bumps days

The most sustained and challenging bumpy sections are found in Les Brevières. The 2 blacks from the top of the Aiguille Percée or Marais chairlifts are lengthy and neither really has an opt-out if you get tired - particularly the Vallon de la Sache, which is the longest black run in the whole ski area. For practise, the red under the Tommeuses chairlift in the Bellevarde area is a decent but relatively short mogul field - and there is often a rut-run down the side of the piste.

powder days

There is so much lift accessed off-piste that you can pretty much go anywhere when there's fresh snow. Popular runs like the Tour du Charvet will generally be tracked by lunchtime, but even relatively obvious spots - for instance under the Tommeuse lift in the Bellevarde sector, or down from the Signals drag in Le Fornet - are so wide open that you will be able to find tracks long after the snow has stopped falling. For a day of off-piste exploration where you can largely go where you want and still end up at a lift at the end, the Solaise area has a lot to offer (➥ solaise).

kids

Though it is often very busy, the appropriately named 'Terrasse' at the top of the Solaise chair/cable car is an excellent area for young children. It is very wide, very flat, has a gentle drag lift, excellent views of the surrounding mountains, and is a short and easy ski to either the Ouilette snack bar or the Datcha restaurant when you need to recharge little legs. The Bellevarde has more green runs, but many of them

have flat sections that will leave children having to pole along.

espace killy tour

Starting and finishing on the Front de Neige, you can cover every sector of the Espace Killy taking only blue runs. On that basis it is an excellent way to spend a day with the family - and if the kids are in ski school you can also ski it on mainly not blue runs. If you start by taking the bus up to Le Fornet, then the cable car and the gondola towards the Chiaupe glacier, you have plenty of time to plan your route for the rest of the day before you get going. One thing you must do is finish the day in La Daille - that way you can stop at the Folie Douce for a celebratory drink and soak up the party atmosphere before you make the ski down, which ends in a superb final schuss.

bad weather

If you can't see anything up high but you still want to ski, your best bet is La Daille. Being below the tree-line keeps the clouds away, so there will still be reasonable on-piste visibility, and if there's been a decent snowfall the powder through the trees will be good. Less convenient but also rather less busy is the ski down to Le Laisinant, in the Solaise area. There's no lift back up, so it's a lengthy round trip, but the 'Super L' (➥ solaise) is one of the few off-piste runs that remain pretty skiable while it's still snowing.

The Espace Killy is a superb off-piste destination - there is a huge amount of open space to suit all levels of powder skiing. Val is home to any number of well-known lines, including the Tour du Charvet and the Cugnaï - and over in Tignes there is the Grande Motte and everything that surrounds it, along with more reachable (though less skiable!) descents like the Tufs couloirs. For any of this you need 2 things - the right equipment and the right company. You should never stray off-piste without an avalanche transceiver, a snow shovel and an avalanche probe, and there's no point in having these things unless you know how to use them. The first thing to do is to get some professional instruction - and just as importantly, when you ski off-piste, go with a guide. For a full description of the off-piste skiing in the Espace Killy, read the Vamos guide 'Val d'Isère - Tignes Off Piste', by Jean-Luc Steiger and Guy Bonnevie, available in bookstores in Val d'Isère and from specialist shops in the UK.

74

henry's avalanche talk

Henry is a chap who knows about avalanches. He write a regular snow report in the Marmotte Times (available free from pretty much every shop and bar in town), and also holds twice weekly talks and courses on how to recognize avalanche danger in the snowpack and how to cope with avalanches if you see one or are caught in one. The talks are held at 6pm at

Dick's Tea Bar, on Tuesdays (an introductory talk) and Thursdays (a more in-depth discussion). Both talks are free and involve video footage and plenty of humour (in the right places!). For some hands on experience, the on-the-mountain courses run on Wednesday and Thursday afternoons, and involve everything you need to know about using your beeper, shovel and probe. An afternoon's instruction will cost around €30.

le tour du charvet

Along with being home to a large number of gentle pistes, the Bellevarde area is also the launching point for the Tour du Charvet, possibly Val's best known - and most skied - off-piste run. It is a long sweeping traverse around the back of the Massif du Charvet, and apart from the fact that is is nowhere near any lifts or piste bashers, it might as well be a piste. It is a wonderful run for both its scenery and the fact that it is eminently skiable. It is lift accessed, and could be skied by someone with only a very little off-piste experience - as such it makes an excellent introduction to the world of proper off-piste skiing. There's nothing steep, and so nowhere for you to get scared or tired, and at the end of it all you come down to the Manchet chairlift in the Solaise sector. If you are a boarder, you should be warned that although you will probably have a few fun turns, a lot of the run is a bit too much like a traverse, and the bottom section is pretty flat.

The run starts from the top of the Grand Pré chairlift, behind the excellent warning sign pointing out that you continue at your own risk.

cugnaï

At the top of the world's slowest chairlift is another excellent but rather too accessible descent. It is a pleasant and never-too-challenging run that is what the French would call 'toujours sur-tracée' - always tracked-out. To find fresh snow you will have to get up (the mountain) pretty early in the morning, but as with the Tour du Charvet, the Cugnaï is fun because it's easy to get to, it isn't scary and it isn't close to any lifts (until you get to the bottom). The descent runs past the warning signs at the top of the Cugnaï chairlift, and has quite a steep entry that can be a little hairy when there's not a lot of snow cover. Once you're going, though, you needn't do much apart from keep your skis parallel and watch the mountains go past.

ski-touring

Ever wondered about the seemingly mad bunch of skiers who walk up pistes as well as down? To the uninitiated it can seem a desparate bid to save on the lift pass, or complete disregard for a perfectly good lift system. This 'sport' is known as ski touring or ski mountaineering - the latter is perhaps a more appropriate name, given the climbing up as well as the skiing down and on a 'tour' you travel from 'a' to 'b'

in the same way as hiking up mountains in summer. Ski touring means you can get to places not accessed by lift and into off-piste territory otherwise hidden from view. And believe it or not there is immense satisfaction after a physically demanding ascent or descent as well as the enjoyment of being amidst the alpine scenery, away from the mêlée of the pistes. Obviously, different equipment is necessary. To climb up slopes you need skis with touring bindings, which unlock to allow the heel to come away from the ski as you step upwards. You also carry 'skins' - now artificial but so called because they were originally seal skins - to attach to the base of the skis during a climb to prevent them from slipping down. Sounds complicated? Any number of the ski schools will be more than happy to show you how (➜ lessons & guiding).

Though the Espace Killy has nothing like the range of touring options that Chamonix has, it still has a huge mountainous area that is a long way from the lifts, and from mini-tours to long loops that take in Paradiski and the 3 Vallées, there is plenty of potential. Unless you're very experienced, however, you can't do any of this without a guide - and they are the best people to talk to about which route would be right for you (➜ lessons & guiding).

Val d'Isère's best known event, the **big day out**, has grown from what was initially a rather small 1 day affair into a huge showpiece that attracts attention and sponsorship from far and wide. Typically staged at the end of February, it consists of a range of snowpark events that involve some of the best talent in the Alps, and a range of parties that involve pretty much everyone in the resort. The athletic side of the equation involves a series of independent competitions that utilise all of what's available in the park (including a boardercross), and anyone can enter anything - though unless you're very talented you'd be better off on the sidelines, and only joining in when the competitors get to the bars. The event revolves around the big air competition, for which a jump is built at the bottom of the infamous Face run, by the Olympique cable car. Though the heats take place in the Bellevarde park, the final uses the jump on the Face, under lights on the evening of the last day of the event. To the spectator this is a little bit like fireworks night - a big crowd of people all standing around with burgers and hot drinks, watching a display which makes everyone go 'oooh' and 'aaah'.. This oooh-ing and aaah-ing is well justified on the whole, as between the winners (who are very impressive) and the losers (who are just as impressive for different reasons), there's lots to watch.

76

Another mostly boarding event is **mix n' fly**, which as the name suggests is about music and big air, and is organised largely by snowboard shop/school Misty Fly. It is kind of a Little Day Out, in that it doesn't attract much media attention, but nonetheless it involves plenty of impressive jumping, crashing and partying in true snowboard event style.

Another thing you're unlikely to want to enter is the **grand raid**, organised by ski school Evolution 2. Consisting of a full day's worth of off-piste skiing, the event runs a kind of random tour of the Espace Killy, with teams of 2 competing for the fastest times down a variety of off-piste lines. The event is well known in skiing circles, and some competitors train for months beforehand - equally some seasonnaires go out on the beer the night before and still enter. This makes for an entertaining mish-mash of ability levels - though make no mistake, unless you are very fit and very comfortable off-piste this is not for you.

Val regularly hosts a stage of the skiing **world cup** - normally in the first part of the racing calendar thanks to Val's generally reasonable snow coverage in the early part of the season. In addition there are a number of smaller events and displays held in the resort - things like torchlit descents, Christmas processions (generally around Christmas time), junior slalom competitions and so on - and thanks to the 1992 Olympics the resort also has a fine Conference Centre which hosts events throughout the year, including classical music concerts. Full details of the programme of events at the Henri Oreiller Centre are available from the tourist office.

One night a week 1 of the short lifts on the Front de Neige stays open until dark, and for a small charge you can do a bit of **night-skiing**, get a vin chaud and an ESF instructor hovering around offering advice and wisecracks. Check at the tourist office for specific details.

Available through many of the ski schools, the Bureau des Guides and also through Killy Sport (t 0479 060514/0479 411001/0613 856477), **snowshoeing** is a fantastic (and strenuous!) alternative to walking or skiing. A pair of tennis-rackets make you surprisingly mobile even on fresh powder, and the routes take you well away from the pistes so you can be sure of a peaceful and different experience. All equipment is provided, and trips range from a quick couple of hours to as long as 6 days - or there is an evening meal option where you leave at 7:30pm and hike up to the Arolay restaurant in Le Fornet (and fortunately catch a shuttle bus back to town).

If the Espace Killy isn't enough for you, Val d'Isère is right on the Italian border and so **heliskiing** (not legal in France) is pretty easy to organise. Most ski schools offer heliskiing, or you can go

direct to the chaps with the choppers, SAF Hélicoptères (t 0479 419349). For the sight without the strain, they also offer panoramic tours for which you don't need to take your skis (but you probably should take your camera).

If you've ever wanted to travel around the ski area like the *pisteurs* do, you can try out **snowmobiling** courtesy of Alaska (t 0479 419003), who are based next to the overpriced restaurant at the top of the Tommeuses chairlift in the Bellevarde sector.

77

the resort

Val has nothing if not a lot of places to get a meal. Among the sizeable range of options, there's plenty of fondue, lots of crêpes and enough boulangeries to feed the 5000. From the definitively gourmet Chalet du Crêt to late night grease at the Tocade, your every desire should be satisfied. Sushi at the Perdrix Blanche, traditional Italian at La Casa Scara... you could eat out every night for weeks and not eat at the same place twice.

The downside to all this is that on the whole the eateries know they have a captive market. The Val d'Isère price mark-up is perhaps most noticeable on your food bill - and though in some places the food is good enough that you won't mind much, there are quite a few very average restaurants in the town, and you may find yourself wondering how it is that cheese and stale bread can possibly cost €20 per person.

80

restaurants

Like many resorts in the French region of Savoie, there is a gross overpopulation of Savoyarde restaurants. Most are much the same as each other, offering similar menus and similar service in similarly touristy 'traditional' surroundings. None are particularly bad, but some stand out as being particularly good. Unlike some ski resorts, most restaurants in Val d'Isère do not operate a two-sitting policy. Some do, but on the whole you will be

---

snapshot
best for...
french service - 1789
french innovation - le bistro des cîmes
where are the french? - la grande ourse
the perfect pizza - le lodge
pas de pizza - la casa scara
domino's pizza - flash pizza
pay the earth - chalet du crêt
feed the earth - la perdrix blanche
save the earth - sur la montagne

able to reserve a table for whatever time you like. Reserving at least a day in advance is a good idea whatever the day, but as there are so many chalets in Val chalet-night off (typically Wednesday) can be very busy indeed, so book your Wednesday table as early as you can. As some of Val's chalet companies run Sunday-Sunday trips, Thursday can also be rather busy.

prices

In the following reviews the restaurants have been graded 1-5 based on the average price per head of a main course, excluding drinks.

£ - less than €10
££ - €10-15
£££ - €16-21
££££ - €22-29
£££££ - €30 or more

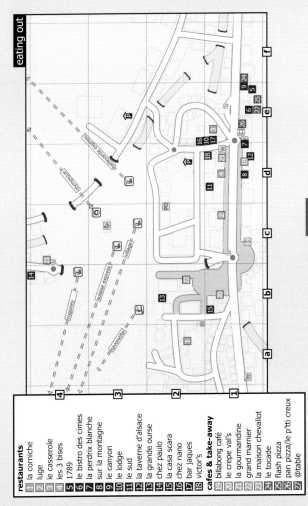

restaurants

1. la corniche
2. luge
3. le casserole
4. les 3 bises
5. 1789
6. le bistro des cimes
7. la perdrix blanche
8. sur la montagne
9. le canyon
10. le lodge
11. le sud
12. la taverne d'alsace
13. la grande ourse
14. chez paulo
15. la casa scara
16. chez nano
17. bar jaques
18. victor's

cafes & take-away

19. billabong café
20. le crepe val's
21. la gourmandine
22. grand marnier
23. la maison chevallot
24. le tocade
25. flash pizza
26. pan pizza/le p'tti creux
27. @table

<< in-town >>

le canyon ££

☎ 0479 061819
🕐 12pm-10pm
🍴 savoyarde & international

In the little cluster of restaurants at the north end of town, the Canyon serves up a decent choice of steaks, fondues, and pizzas in a noisy and sometimes rowdy atmosphere. With plenty of long tables and not much space to hide, it is as good a choice for groups as it is a poor one for romantics - though unless you are looking for privacy (or the toilets) you can't go too far wrong. The Canyon isn't somewhere that worries much about the temperature of the house red, and at the expensive end of the menu you could eat better elsewhere, but for the most part it is not over-priced and there are set-price menus available for those wanting lots of courses without complicating the bill.

82

1789 ££

☎ 0479 061789
🕐 6pm-10pm
🍴 french

In the same building as the Canyon, but as about as far removed from it as possible. 1789 is a truly French place, and though they speak good English if they need to, this is one spot where English is definitely not the first language. Service is superb throughout, and rather outshines the food, which though fine is nothing to write home about.

la corniche ££££

☎ 0479 061875
🕐 12pm-2pm, 7pm-10pm
🍴 savoyarde & international

Though it looks sweet and cosy from the outside, La Corniche is a surprisingly large and open restaurant that can seat 100 at capacity. Despite being a short walk away from the beaten track, it is always busy and - as with most places - has a very English client base. The non-fondue food is available à la carte or in a variety of set-price menus - including vegetarian and gourmet options - and all dishes are reliably well-prepared and presented, with the emphasis falling on good food and good atmosphere.

le casserole £££

☎ 0479 411571
🕐 7pm-10:30pm
🍴 traditional savoyarde

A dark and at first sight rather dingy feeling restaurant that at times can be a little too overtly unenthusiastic about serving fondue to foreigners. Equally, if you time it right or come in a large group it can be quite a jolly place, and the wide range of Savoyarde specialities are all well enough presented. It's a perfectly good spot to while away an evening with some cheese, but don't expect to be blown away. The best thing about it is that it is easy to find.

luge £££

p81
c1

☎ 0479 066939
🕐 7pm-10pm
🍴 traditional savoyarde

Under the wing of the Blizzard hotel, the Luge shares the same warm wood and cosy feel of its parent, and combines intelligent and deferential service with outstanding food to make it quite the best place in town to line your stomach with cheese. The Savoyarde style menu feels somehow more genuine here, the food is less about fancy presentation and more about eating well, and there is something gentle and delicate about the décor which makes eating in the Luge a relaxing experience. It is all quietly French, and even when full it is unlikely to be too rowdy... the Luge offers neither pomp nor circumstance, just simple fine dining.

la gourmandine £

p81
c4

☎ 0479 411111
🕐 10am-8pm
🍴 crêpes

A small establishment which is largely a daytime crêperie, the Gourmandine features here by virtue of staying open 3 evenings a week to cope with the Rond-Point restaurant shortage. The menu is

pizzas, crepes, tartiflette and the odd fondue, and the surroundings are similarly simple and unthreatening - but it is a friendly place and one which will take a group booking for the entire restaurant.

les 3 bises ££

p81
d1

☎ 0479 060493
🕐 3pm-11pm
🍴 traditional savoyarde & crêpes

A small and informal fondue shop with a simple and unsurprising menu. The food is not expensive, and though you won't be blown away by the creativity of the place, it has an unthreatening and not-too-English allure which to some will come as a welcome relief from the King's Road bustle on the streets outside. It is open for crêpes in the afternoon, and the most popular evening option is 'la formule', a set menu with a choice of most of the à la carte dishes, with a glass of house wine and a coffee thrown in. And if you need further entertaining after you eat, Club 21 is only a yard away.

83

la perdrix blanche £££

p81
d1

☎ 0479 061209
🕐 4pm-11pm
🍴 international

With a random mish-mash of international cuisine and a huge throughput of food and people, the Perdrix Blanche is one of the busiest and most diverse restaurants in Val. It specialises in fish, and one night a week offers sushi alongside the standard offerings - and on other nights you can get curry, pizza, Mexican, some Savoyarde food and various other dishes. There is also a wide range of desserts on offer, cleverly placed so that you have to walk past them to get to any of the tables. The restaurant extends as far as the eye can see, seating 200 and regularly hitting capacity. Having 20 waiters running around means service is a little unpredictable and it all feels a little factory produced, but there are some things (like fish) that the Perdrix does better than anywhere else at the price.

84

la grande ourse ££££

☎ 0479 060019
🕐 11am-10pm
🍴 international

With a gourmet menu and a perfect slopeside location, La Grande Ourse offers a warm welcome and fantastic food to anyone not too attached to their bank balance. The French owners are well attuned to catering for a clientele that in high season can be up to 90% English, and the range of dishes is enough to amuse the mouth of even the most demanding gourmand - though the kitchen can also cope with cheeseburger and chips... for the kids of course. Right on the Front de Neige, at lunch you can ski to your table (assuming you've

reserved one) - and if you're searching for somewhere for a special soirée you needn't look any further.

le lodge ££

☎ 0479 060201
🕐 6pm-11pm
🍴 international

Above the excellent Lodge bar lies the equally popular and unpretentious Lodge restaurant, a casual sort of place that is perfect for an informal beer-and-pizza meal. The layout is a little clumsy, and aside from the pizza and the set-price menu, some of the food is a touch dear for what it is - some dishes cost much the same as at the culinarily superior Luge... but as with the bar downstairs, the main attraction of the Lodge is its informally noisy atmosphere. That and the excellent spring roll starters.

la casa scara ££££

☎ 0479 062621
🕐 6pm-10pm
🍴 traditional italian

As authentic an Italian as you could hope to find on the French side of the border, and one of the best restaurants in Val. In traditional style, the food is arranged into 4 courses, with 2 rounds of main dishes, and the wine list is selected to fit with the menu. Risotto is a speciality, but you can't really miss whatever you choose: all the ingredients are excellent quality, all are imported from Italy - and though the owner is Val d'Isère born and bred, he knows his Brunello from his Barolo. Being a couple of steps into the old Val village the Casa has plenty of old-stone-building charm, and if you're looking to escape fondue saturation, this is the best choice in town. Just don't go hoping for a pizza, because they don't serve it.

le sud	£££

☎ 0479 419542
🕐 6pm-11pm
✗ mediteranean

p81 d1 11

Hidden away on the first level of one of the shopping galleries, Le Sud is a relatively new place which has tried to find a niche in the overcrowded Val restaurant scene. It is spacious and relaxed, has a separate lounge area with comfy coffee sofas, a separate seating area for those who want to eat a little less formally, and it somehow manages to attract a predominantly 30something crowd. The menu is quite light, in a couscous kind of way, the emphasis falling more on taste than on filling you up, and though it doesn't quite challenge the leaders of the pack, the Sud is a different eating experience that is well worth a try.

le bistro des cîmes	££

☎ 0479 061797
🕐 6pm-10pm
✗ international

p81 e1 6

A funny sort of place with simple menus and simple pricing that take the faff out of restaurant food. The booth-style seating arrangements are rather unusual, in a round-the-corner sort of way that actually works well once you're sitting. The food has a modernist slant - that is to say that there are no fiddly sauces or confusing dishes, just an uncomplicated and very good quality range of dishes with influences from Provence and Asia. Being on one edge of the cramping and unattractive Gallerie des Cimes, it isn't in the most sensible of spaces and you'll probably wonder where it all is when you get there, but eating at the Bistro is a rather different and very satisfying way to spend an evening.

85

victor's	££

☎ 0479 060652
🕐 10am-11pm
✗ swedish & international

p81 d1 18

An innovative and rightly very popular restaurant that operates a pic n' mix style menu, from which you choose the different bits of your main course individually. The food ranges from Swedish specialities to a varied list of international choices, all of which are very reasonably priced. Not surprisingly the clientele has a Scandinavian bias, so you shouldn't be surprised if the table next to yours breaks into a loud medley of singing and drinking... but this all adds to the atmosphere, and if you need something to take the edge off, the adjoining bar is perfect for a pre- or post-dinner cocktail.

sur la montagne £ £

☎ 0619 580521
🕐 10am-10:30pm
🍴 savoyarde & french

p81 d1 | 8

An approachable and friendly place that functions as salon de thé during daylight hours and restaurant once the sun's gone down. It is quite new, and feels it, but in a rustic way that fits with the inexpensive food (by Val standards) and service that is neither tired nor cynical in its welcome. Sur la Montagne prides itself in its use of regional produce, and the menu blends Savoyarde food with a range of other French influences. You will be neither blown away nor let down by the food - the attraction of Sur la Montagne is its atmosphere, which as with its décor is unashamedly simple and relaxed. In a word, it is pleasant, and if you like black pudding this is the place to go.

86

and the rest

Of the other options the best is the lovely **etable d'alain** (t 0479 411085), an authentic farm just out of the southern end of town (left at the first roundabout you reach). **chez nano** (t 0479 061841), next to the Lodge offers pleasingly cheap pizzas and steaks. On the other side of the Lodge is **bar jaques** (t 0479 060389), a restaurant-cum-bar that is most notable for operating a no smoking policy throughout. The main option up at the Rond Point des Pistes is **chez paolo** (t 0479 062804), a large place with a large bar and a large selection of pizzas and pastas, fondue and the like.

<< further afield >>

le chalet du crêt £££££

☎ 0479 062077
🕐 6:30m-11pm
🍴 french

val d'isère

la daille

It is not uncommon for holidaymakers to reserve their table at the Chalet de Crêt before even booking their flights and accommodation - as well known to fine diners as Bananas is to drinkers, Such is its reputation in some circles it has been dubbed the 'Chalet de World Dêbt'... it is certainly expensive, but the price assures you excellent gourmet food with service to match. Beautifully furnished and cleverly arranged over 2 levels, it feels at once spacious and intimate, and the high level of return customers (around 70% of its clientele) is testament to superb quality and attention to detail in every aspect of its trade. If you can face the walk or can find a taxi, a meal at the Crêt is one you will remember as long as you remember the rest of your trip.

les clochetons £££

☎ 0479 411311
🕐 9am-9:30pm
✕ savoyarde & french

A large chalet building that is halfway between mountain restaurant and evening diner. About 400 yards up past the Rond-Point, it is a slog to get to unless you book in advance and make use of their shuttle. Lunch is pricey and plat du jour based, with fondues in bad weather. Food is good and the restaurant is cleverly placed at the point you run out of speed on the long schuß down from Santons. Evenings are semi-gastro in style, with a choice of menus that cram in more courses the more you pay.

l'arolay ££

☎ 0479 061168
🕐 11am-11pm
✕ traditional savoyarde

Far enough out of town to escape the Val d'Isère price inflation and superior to many of the restaurants you can walk to, l'Arolay is frequented by those for whom food, friendly service and a good view top the priority list. It has its own free shuttle service from and back to town that runs early evening through until midnight - you book this when you reserve your table. The midday menu is a plat du jour affair, in which the humour of the place is reflected by the once a week offering 'according to the chef's mood' (!) - no Val d'Isère pretension here. Evenings are in the Savoyarde format, and though the range of food isn't huge it is underpriced and comes with fireplace and genuine homely welcome, things that are conspicuously absent from some of the more manufactured and cynical spots in town.

eating out

cafés

There are all sorts of places in Val d'Isère to grab a quick bite or to drink a slow coffee or to generally escape from the sometimes too hectic après. Crêpes are almost as traditional as fondue in ski resorts, and there is certainly no shortage of pancake shops - also there a variety of cafés and tea rooms that sell pastries, chocolates and generally snacky food, and most are open over the lunchtime siesta. In most cases crêpes are crêpes, a pizza slice is a pizza slice, and coffee is coffee - but there are some places that for one reason or another are a touch more memorable than the average.

le crêpe val's £

☎ 0479 411462
🕐 2pm-10pm
✕ crêpes

A small and beautiful place that is as much tea room or restaurant as it is crêperie, the curiously apostrophised Crêpe Val's is one of Val d'Isère's mini-delights. Amongst quaint wooden décor and cutesy chairs you can choose from an enormous range of sweet and savoury crêpes, and also salads, fondue, raclette, pasta, steaks and full blown 3-course menus - so much in fact that it's hard to believe they can fit all the ingredients into such a tiny kitchen. It doesn't feel tacky, it is too small ever to get too busy, and the friendly welcome is a genuine one.

billabong coffee shop £

☎ 0479 060954
🕐 10am-10pm
✕ burgers & snacks

Through the back of the Billabong and Quiksilver stores, the Billabong café is a chilled out American-style diner which serves processed burgers and oversweet hot chocolate. The main reason to go there is the large TV screen and the no-smoking policy, which combine to mean you can eat without coughing and watch extreme sports as you chew.

la maison chevallot £

☎ 0479 062936
🕐 8am-8pm
✕ pastries & pizza (& bread)

A salon de thé in a bakery, the Maison Chevallot offers an array of freshly baked breads and homemade pastries, pies, quiches and so on, along with posh chocolates for the sweet-toothed skier... it is a friendly and rather small place which is most notable for its no-smoking policy and the fact that you can get a more substantial and less expensive slice of hot pizza here than in either the P'tit Creux or Pan Pizza.

late night & take-away

Despite the huge range of restaurants, there are any number of reasons to want take-away. If you fancy eating standing up you have plenty of choices for a quick bite at any time during daylight hours - though as with the cafés most of the take-away food outlets are much of a muchness. For food after curfew, the choices are rather fewer, and if you don't like pizza there's really only one place to go.

@table £££

☎ 0479 419998
🕐 6pm-11pm
🍴 international

If the self-catering kitchen looks like too much of an effort - or if the shops shut before you got to them and you don't fancy eating out - @table have the solution. They deliver a wide range of decent and inexpensive food to wherever you are: things like boeuf bourguignon, duck confit, a range of curries, spare ribs and so on... they will also bring round beer and wine, meaning you can still have a proper meal no matter how disorganised or lazy you're feeling.

les 3 bises (crêpes) £

☎ -
🕐 3pm-8pm
🍴 crêpes

A small hut outside the front of the 3 Bises restaurant, this is milk, egg and flour at its take away best. The menu is standard crêpes and galettes, there's nowhere to sit - and nowhere to stand - but for a friendly smile and a crêpe on the run, this is the best place in town.

flash pizza £

☎ 0479 419606
🕐 5pm-11pm
🍴 pizza

The Val d'Isère version of Domino's, Flash Pizza serves a range of pizzas to take away, which for a small additional charge they'll deliver to you. This works whether you're stuck in your apartment and can't be bothered to move or stuck in the Saloon and don't want to leave. The pizzas are good, the toppings liberal, and most importantly the delivery service knows its way around: Val isn't a big enough place for you to have to describe where you are.

pan pizza/le p'tit creux £

☎ -
🕐 11am-2am
🍴 pizza

These are in fact 2 entirely separate establishments, but they're right next to each other and are more or less identical. They are your most obvious choices for take-away pizza, and both sell slices and full-scale pizzas of much the same

89

standard and from much the same menu. If there's a queue at one, go to the other. If there's a queue at both, walk for half a minute to Flash or the Maison Chevallot.

le tocade

☎ 0479 411541
🕓 10am-4am
🍴 kebabs & burgers

p81
f1

At the northern extent of town, Val d'Isère's only kebab shop is the best place to satisfy your cravings for grease and the only place to get food after 2am. They also sell sandwiches and baguettes, and the small terrace is a popular sunny afternoon hangout. The staff are well accustomed to drunken English - indeed they don't all speak much French - and they tend to stay open until the last post-Dick's stragglers have crawled past.

grand marnier

☎ 0479 411037
🕓 11am-8pm
🍴 crêpes

p81
b2

Next to the lift pass office on the Front de Neige, Grand Marnier is a ski-in crêperie that is the perfect pre-après snack stop - as long as you like Grand Marnier. They presumably have some sort of contractual obligation to include their chosen liqueur in everything they sell - you will have difficulty even getting a hot chocolate au naturel - but if you like your orange flavoured liqueur, this is your spot. There is no table service and cramped seating makes getting to and from the bar in ski boots a bit of challenge, but the crêpes are tasty and not too dear.

90

après-ski & nightlife

Arguably more famous than the surrounding ski area, Val d'Isère's nightlife is as vibrant and varied as you could possibly hope for. In busy weeks you'll be hard pressed to find a quiet corner, but aside from that there is something for everyone - and though it may take a bit of wandering around before you work out which place suits you best, whatever your taste you'll find a home somewhere. The common denominators are loud music and lots of people, and their multiple incarnations make Val d'Isère one of the best après destinations in the Alps.

92

bars & pubs

The first thing to be aware of is the **pub crawl** night. Typically held on a Monday, this is when all the large tour operators organise a group crawl around pre-designated bars, winding up at Dick's Tea-Bar. If you're lucky enough to be on one of these organised binges you will encounter a policy of bars giving away free shots with each drink you buy - 1 drink and 1 shot per bar, and probably 5 or so bars until you get to Dick's. If you're unlucky enough to get caught up in one of these binges when you thought you were just going for a quiet pint, you can rest assured in the knowledge that after one or two quick drinks they will all disappear just as quickly as they appeared.

There are lots of chalets in the resort, so the next **busy** night on the agenda is Wednesday, when the chalet staff

> **snapshot**
>
> **après...**
> king's road cocktails - café face
> the student union - lounge bar
> cramped but cool - lodge bar
>
> **après après...**
> chalet girls & army officers - banana's
> nordic warriors - le petit danois
> french funk - bentley's
>
> **and dawn-breakers**
> english fumbling - dick's tea bar
> french frolicking - club 21

generally take their night off and go drinking. Since Val tour operators run a number of Sunday transfers, Thursday night can also be a hot spot. As with the pub crawl, this is a recommendation or a warning, depending on your disposition. On the whole, however, it doesn't much matter what night(s) you go out on. Unless you have impeccably bad timing, most of the bars in town will be busy. The only night this is not so likely to be true is the first night in resort, when many people decide to try to have at least 1 day's skiing without a hangover - by sleeping off the transfer with an early night.

prices

You should expect to pay €10ish for a pitcher of beer, with cocktails, 'pints' and wine more or less at London prices.

93

bars
1. le saloon
2. bentley's
3. the moris pub
4. pacific
5. café face
6. the lodge bar
7. victor's
8. the lounge bar
9. le petit danois
10. banana's
11. café fats
12. XV
13. la fôret

clubs
14. dick's tea bar
15. club 21

banana's £

☎ 0450 060423

🕐 10am-1:30am

🍴 burgers, tex-mex etc

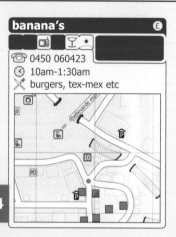

Bananas is something of a Val d'Isère institution, with a reputation that runs the length of London's King's Road. Anyone who has been to Val is likely to have spent some time in here, and everyone who has been will have an opinion on the place. It is popular during the day by virtue of having a great snacky menu in the ground level restaurant, which serves a variety of food ranging from snacks, burgers and tex-mex through to proper three course evening meals, but the true Bananas is more concerned with the other side of the food and drink equation. Drinks prices vary curiously depending on whether you're upstairs or down, and while the restaurant section is perfect for anything through until early evening, the downstairs bar is the destination of choice post 8pm. It is an argument for atmosphere over practicality - a variety of pokey corners give it a pretty cramped feel, but the loud and (generally) young crowd of chalet girls and army officers makes for a cosy early evening and a hectic and drunken late night that is quintessentially Val d'Isère. English is the first language on both sides of the bar, and though the famous vodka freestyles will damage both your liver and your wallet, if you're hankering for a party there can be few better places.

la forêt

☎ 0479 060427
🕓 4pm-2am

In Val's Scandinavian quarter, la Forêt is a little detached from the main nightlife, but is nonetheless a cool and surprisingly large bar that is well worth the hike out from the centre. Pool, table football, a projection tv screen for sports and a stage for - amongst other things - karaoke, all in an atmosphere that is rather more friendly than some of the more central drinking holes. La Forêt adopts the same by-the-hour drinks pricing policy as Café Face - but you don't have to fight to get to the bar or dress up posh to feel like you fit in.

la forêt

☎ 0479 060427
🕓 4pm-2am

Small, dark, and funky, the Lodge is one of the best small bars in Val d'Isère. It's too loud to be relaxing and too little to fit a pool table or a pub crawl group - but if your evening inclinations are based more on atmosphere than pints of beer, the Lodge delivers in a slightly offbeat way that doesn't aim itself at any particular social group. Skiers, boarders, holidaymakers, locals... the mix of clientele is neither particularly English nor overwhelmingly foreign, and similarly does not fit into any particular age bracket. You will know as soon as you go

in whether or not it is the place for you - and if you like it, you may find yourself there every night of your stay.

the lounge bar

☎ -
🕓 4pm-2am

If you're hankering after your university days, the Lounge takes a very good shot at recreating a student union bar. There's , regular live music, pool and table football, a large projection tv that shows Sky sports, cheap(ish) drinks, 5 internet stations around the corner... but also that intangible **95** something in the air that makes you feel like you've got an essay deadline at the end of the week. It's a big space which fills like a sardine tin when there's a live band, and on quieter nights (or during the day) is a fine place to drink a coffee and go through your lecture notes.

café face

☎ 0479 062980
🕓 3pm-2am

Catering for a slightly more refined crowd than some of the Val drinking holes, the Face is a cocktail bar with a comfy chic feel that will put London twentysomethings instantly at ease. It's best to get there early - partly because you're much more likely to get a seat, and partly because the drinks get gradually more expensive by the hour (hence the clock in the doorway). They don't serve anything hot. No coffee sipping in here. The music is loud, funky, and often features saxophonists wandering disconcertingly around the room - and if you feel the need to take a step down the social ladder, Dick's is just across the road.

pacific

☎ 0479 062919
🕐 3pm-2am

p93 b1 · 4

Down the stairs round the side of Precision, Pacific is by turns chilled and comfy, loud and rowdy, or jammed full of football fans. Five plasma screen tvs draw capacity crowds on game nights - and there is comprehensive coverage of any game you might want to watch... but away from the pitch, Pacific is a big open space that is as perfect for a relaxed early evening game of pool as it is for a late night drinking session. There's a weekly raffle in which you can win a pair of skis - cleverly the tickets come when you spend a certain amount on drink - and this combined with regular theme nights ensures a hectic dance-on-the-thankfully-low-tables atmosphere that's always more welcoming than not.

the moris pub

☎ 0479 062211
🕐 3pm-2am

p93 b1 · 3

One of the best known bars in Val, and as live music goes one of the best locations in the Alps. It's a very large and rather dark pub-style place that will either appeal to you or won't - there's no TV so no live sports, there's a live band every night so no peace and quiet (except in early evening), but for songs you can sing along to there's nowhere better. When the main bar's service isn't up to speed there's a second option by the entrance, and the Moris boasts a dangerously drinkable toffee vodka. With enough standing space to jump around and enough round-the-corner seating to hide yourself away, if you like your tunes played live you'll find your comfort here.

le saloon

☎ 0479 060158
🕐 4pm-2am

p93 b2 · 1

Right on the Front de Neige, the Saloon is ski-in ski-out après is busy from last lift to last orders. In spite of its large size it seems to be almost always full, and the low-ceilings make it a very hot and smoky place to be. But this, even combined with sofas stolen from your Grandma's front room, is not enough to put off the crowds, and with pool tables and ample seating, 3 bars and a pseudo-dancefloor, the Saloon is a great place to shed the cold weather blues. Other benefits include doorstaff who double as ski police, keeping an eye on the rack so no one walks off with your new pair of Bandits.

96

victor's

☎ 0479 060652
🕐 12pm-2am

A Swedish version of a cocktail shop, the bar half of Victor's is a blend of excellent staff and too many orders: it caters for the restaurant as well as the drinkers, and so even when it's quiet you may have to wait around before getting served. The general feel is unpretentiously alcoholic, and the window seats are perfect for watching people fall over on the ice outside... it's not a big place, and if you time it wrong you may not even be able to get in the door, but if you can find a niche Victor's is a great place to down your weeks wages in true Scandy spirit.

bentley's

☎ 0479 066213
🕐 4pm-1:30am

If Bananas represents one extreme of the Val social scene, Bentley's holds the other corner. It contradicts every Val stereotype: the clientele is mostly French and mostly seasonnaires, the music is mostly reggae, drum & bass and the like, the tv screen will as likely show cartoons as football or extreme sports... it is a very welcoming and friendly bar, with a pool table, 6 cheap internet stations, free Playstation 2, and interesting wall decorations - but as with Bananas it is an acquired taste. If you're wondering where

the dreadlocked snowboarder crowd hang out, Bentley's is the place - and anyone for whom the rowdy English are a little hard to bear will feel right at home.

XV

☎ 0479 419055
🕐 4pm-1:30am

As the names suggests, XV has a rugby theme. But while there is a large tv that does show rugby, you're unlikely to see too many England shirts - it is a French run, French staffed bar that displays a variety of largely French rugby memorabilia. Drinks all have rugby names, so you'll find yourself drinking 'le maul' or 'le drop' - but it is understated enough that if you weren't looking for it you could miss the rugby side of things altogether. Between the bizarre bucket seats and the wandering dog it is a friendly and welcoming place, but in a very French way. No sign of Woodward or Wilkinson in here - anyone venting the lungs with a rendition of Swing Low does so at their own risk.

97

café fats

☎ -
🕐 10am-1am

As English a place as you will find, Fats is an all-day greasy spoon hangout which becomes a bar in the evenings. Along with bacon and eggs breakfast they serve butties, fish fingers, jacket potatoes and so on, and if the weather's bad Fats is a fine place to while away an hour watching Sky sports on the tv - though there's no comfy seating, so it's not quite the spot to curl up with a hot chocolate. At night time it is as lively as it is chilled during the day - although it is not to be confused with the nominally similar Café Face.

le petit danois

☎ 0479 062797
🕑 9am-2am

p93
e2

98 Set back a little from the main road and bemusingly difficult for some to find, the Danois is ostensibly a Danish bar. This is true inasmuch as it employs a number of Danes, but the barmen tend to be anything but petit, they serve full English breakfast (in what is a very good restaurant section), and the clientele is as international as it comes. It is not instantly welcoming, and it is a fine place to avoid on the weekend when it functions as a cargo bay for a number of Scandanavian tour operators... but it is one of the few bars in Val that will be busy regardless of the football/rugby schedule, and it is equally good for a game of pool in the afternoon or a lively night on the Amstel.

and the rest

This is not the full extent of the enjoyment available. If you're walking in to town from out towards Le Crêt or La Daille, you can stop and have a game of

pool with proper elbow room at **simon's café**, which is not a café at all. If you're actually all the way out in La Daille, **l'armoise** (t 0479 060344) is a good sized bar that makes up the majority of the après scene. There are some others in town too - out of the back of the Gallerie des Cîmes is the best hidden bar in the resort, **le pub** (t 0479 060140). For a curious and rather French experience try **boubou's** (t 0479 062215), in between the Front de Neige and the main roundabout. And for a beer or two with some live music in a more French vein, try the **warm up** (t 0479 062700), which is also home to Val's third nightclub.

nightclubs

Val has possibly the most infamous nightclub in the Alps - amongst English skiers at least. The Dick's Tea Bar in Val is the original - and probably still the best though the other members of the clan in Méribel and Chamonix may beg to differ. The infamous bar/club could lay a decent claim to being 'where it all started' - and it has been going strong ever since. Consequently clubbing in Val is not quite the typical ski resort experience. Dick's is an altogether more English night out - so much so that you may forget you're in the Alps and think that you are in any one of Fulham's late night venues.

Dick's is only one of the 3 places open after 2am - the others being the more French Club 21 and the more often closed than not Warm Up. Where you end up will probably be determined by where, and when, you started.

prices

Cover charges vary, normally depending on what time you arrive and how late you are - but it's a small price to pay to get out of the nighttime chill. Cloakrooms also levy a minimal fee - but the clubs make their money from drinks prices, which are significantly higher than in the bars.

dick's tea bar

☎ 0479 061487
◷ 4pm-4am

p93
d/e2

The Val Dick's Tea Bar functions as an après bar, and opens its doors in time to catch people as they walk past on their way down from the slopes. Afternoons and evenings are subject to a happy hour that pulls the otherwise clubby prices roughly in line with the other bars, and there are occasionally live bands and comedians organised to pull in the punters. Later on Dick's puts on its clubbing hat. Clientele is about three-quarters English, and if you're there after midnight the chances are that about three-quarters of the clientele will have had one or two too many. This is the whole point though - late-night Dick's isn't classy, it's drunken. There are theme nights in a 'pimps and prostitutes' kind of way, and a 'VIP' room in which you have to either buy a bottle of spirits or be a seasonnaire. Lots of jolly

Englishmen (and women), a very standard array of appeal-to-everyone pop and club tunes, nothing to do tomorrow except run around on the snow... it's a proven cocktail for success.

club 21

☎ 0479 060493
◷ 10pm-4am

p93
d1

Club 21, also known as Vingt-et-Un, is French in every way that Dick's is English. It is a much smaller place, and somehow also manages to have much shorter queues. It feels much more like a club inside, and certainly much more like a French club. People still drink lots, but there is less of the downing of pints. People still dance lots, but generally to a much more clubby style of music. People will still try to chat you up in a drunken fashion, but probably not in such an arrogant way. You can still try to chat people up, but the chances are that if try to do it in English you will get negative responses. Even ordering at the bar is best done in 'deux bières' fashion. You will know instantly whether you are better off here or in Dick's. Horses for courses.

99

overview

To most Espace Killy holidaymakers, St. Foy is just the name of one of those towns you pass through on your transfer to resort. It's about 15 minutes up the road from Bourg St. Maurice, and there's not much there apart from a shop or two and some pleasant-looking buildings. For those who know, however, this little village signals the turn off for St. Foy *station*, a small and - until recently - largely overlooked resort that boasts 1 bar, a few restaurants, 3 lifts, and some of the best off-piste around.

St. Foy is not La Grave. It doesn't have endless extreme skiing lines and no pistes at all - rather there is a tiny pisted network (a good skier could ski every piste in about 2 hours) and a tiny community of locals and seasonnaires and regular holidaymakers, all of whom like life a little quieter than it is up the road in Val d'Isère or Tignes. But 'tiny' is now giving way to commercial investment from accommodation giants like MGM and Century 21, and it won't be long until St. Foy's resort is twice its current size - and more disappointingly there is likely soon to be a fourth lift built, accessing off-piste lines that for the moment you have to hike to get to.

getting started

Though not as cheap these days as it was, **accommodation** in St. Foy still costs markedly less than anything higher up the valley in the Espace Killy. There are some apartments (and some more currently being built), but the resort is mostly made up of chalets. A good number of these are privately owned, and frustratingly empty for much of the season (many have been bought as much for the investment as for the skiing). The tourist office (t 0479 069601) keeps a record of all the available accommodation, and there is a Central Reservations Bureau (t 0479 069522) who will give provide you with full information and contact details for what is available.

The **lift pass** office is right on the snow, at the end of the lower level of the walkway. Options for lift passes are about as simple as they come, as there's not much to buy a pass for. An Espace Killy pass of 6 days or more gets you 50% off the price of skiing here - though the pass is so cheap that that isn't as much of an incentive as you might think. The only **ski school** is a mini branch of the ESF (t 0479 069676).

the skiing

There is a small drag in the resort for absolute beginners, and above that 3 lifts lead up the mountain in single file, with the runs becoming progressively harder the higher you go. Snow conditions are less reliable at such a low altitude, especially in early season (when there may be none at all) and in late season (when grass starts popping up all over the pistes). There's enough

100

pisted skiing to keep you happy for a weekend or so - and the blacks at the top may take you longer than that to master - but the real reason to come is for the powder.

The north face of the Fogliettaz may be less well known than other skiable north faces (like the Bellecôte in La Plagne, or the Grande Motte above Tignes), but the descent is no less enjoyable (and possibly more enjoyable, for having less skiers on it). It is not a particularly challenging run as off-piste runs go, but it is still in places both steeper and much more technically demanding than any black run you may have skied. Make no mistake - the Fogliettaz is proper off-piste skiing - unpatrolled, unmarked, and unsafe unless you are skiing with a guide. Once you have a friendly professional on board, you have about an hour's hike from the top lift to get to the launch point, followed by a descent that is as untainted as pretty much anything you can find in the Alps. The runs finishes in the tiny hamlet of La Mazure - you can't ski back round to St. Foy, so make sure you organise some transport before you leave (your guide will be full of ideas for this).

the resort
For now, it is all quaintly small (if you can see past the construction sites). There are 2 ski shops - a Ski Set and the independent and well-stocked Zigzags - and a small Sherpa supermarket. The bar, **la pitchouli** (t 0479 062574),

is as small and friendly as the resort it's in, in part because it serves a local brew that tips the scales at 7.5%. There are 2 restaurants on the strip - **le bec de l'ane** (t 0479 069245) is a pizzeria, and new in winter 2004 is **chez allison**. If they aren't your kettle of fish you can hike across the snow to **la maison à colonnes** (0479 069480), which is a traditional Savoyarde place with traditionally grumpy service.

Most people will probably never get around to going to St Foy - this is just as well, as it isn't a very big place. But for those that have discovered it and discovered that they like it, it is the perfect ski destinnation. And even if one bar and a handful of pistes doesn't sound like your cup of tea, it's still worth bearing in mind for when there's lots of snow but also lots of clouds.

101

Away from the pistes, Val's attractions fall largely into one of two categories: sporting or relaxation. From bakery and bridge to ice karting and parapenting, there is bound to be something to keep you happy if the lifts are closed or you lose your skis.

more exercise?

The **swimming pool** on the Front de Neige (t 0479 060590) is open 2pm-7pm every day but Saturday. It is heated and a decent size - 25m - and they also have a sauna and steam bath.

102

If your summer passion is for **rock climbing**, you will be able to keep your crimping fingers in shape on a pretty impressive wall in the sports centre (t 0479 060349) next to the Henri Oreiller conference centre. This **sports hall** also caters for badminton, basketball, table tennis, gymnastics, five-a-side football, and generally anything you could play in a sports hall.

Assuming there is good-ish weather, the mini **ice rink** on the Front de Neige is open (2pm-7pm, and until 10pm on Wednesdays) for general circling and falling over, along with occasional curling and ice-football contests. Afternoons and evenings, with the sporting side of affairs starting at 7pm.

On the northern edge of town is an **ice karting** circuit (t 0479 062140/0611 958000, i circuitval.com) which hosts

various different types of vehicular races throughout the day and evening (10am-12pm, 2pm-8pm depending on weather conditions). The standard offering is effectively like go-karting, but you can also race quad bikes, ski-doos and clapped-out old Panda 4x4s. Reserve before you go.

To exercise a different set of muscles try a work-out with Patrick Chevallot, an award-winning pastry chef. Based at L'Adroit Bakery (t 0479 061609), among the variety of delights on offer is a twice a week (Tuesdays and Thursdays) **bakery class** given by the master chef, dealing with anything from making bread to crafting fine tartes and stodgy cakes. Just out of the south end of town the Ferme is a short walk from the centre, and within skipping distance from the Train Rouge bus stop.

sky high

The upwards version of parachuting, **parapenting** (or 'parascending') is available in the Bellevarde area (and elsewhere on request) through a number of ski schools (➝ lessons & guiding) and some private teachers (t 0609 466478, t 0662 106673 or Eric Wyss on t 0686 963124). All jumps are tandem with an instructor, so all you have to do is sit in a big sleeping bag and watch the world slip by.

For a rather different look at the ski area - and a more peaceful and intimate flight than the helicopter option - you can hop on a **microlight**. The launching point is the top of the Olympique cable car (t 0607 224397)

inner calm

The Village des Enfants up by the Solaise cable car is home to a **bridge** tournament every evening (5pm everyday) participation generally by reservation only (t 0688 076395).

yoga classes (t 0479 402639/0603 106395) run 3 evenings every week, also in the Village des Enfants. Classes are dual-language and once a week are in English only, so you can relax your brain too. Private bookings are also available on request.

For those who feel the need for a bit of pampering after a hard day on the slopes, there is a baffling array of **spa treatments** available throughout the town or in the comfort of your own chalet. Much in the same vein as a London beauty salon, Paul Berrard on the Place de l'Office de Tourisme (t 0479 060037/0479 060171) offers a range of skin treatments along with pricey haricuts and posh perfumes. Institut Anne Gallien (centre medical t 0479 419250, 0684 481466) has probably most expansive (and most expensive) range of beauty services in the town: tanning, waxing, facials, skin treatments, manicures, massage... all of which are available slightly cheaper when taken in combination. Upstairs in the Galerie du Thovex to the right of the Tourist Office, Therapeos (t 0479

419677) is a large gym and beauty place, open 10am-12:30pm, 3pm-8:15pm for massages, saunas and so on. You could spend a night in a decent hotel for the price of 90 minutes of manual lymphatic drainage - though the two are probably equally recuperative. Sidney Voet (t 0613 893714) is an independent masseur who relieves even the hassle of having to get to the clinic, With a simple mobile massage service so you can enjoy a half-hour's relaxation without having to leave your chalet. Based in the Hotel Savoy, SkiFys (t 0617 810631) is a Danish sports massage outfit who are more attuned to skiing-related strains than they are to manicures and head massages. They also operate an injury assessment clinic and have basic ultrasound physio facilities - and a portable massage bed in case you don't feel like moving.

A number of the top-end hotels, such as the Barmes and the Blizzard) have a **fitness and health club** which non-residents can use for a small fee.

culture vulture

The high concentration of English in Val ensures the **cinema** has regular VO showings (*Version Originale* - which means an English version). The films change every night, and releases fall more or less in line with what's on in the cinema back home. There is a film at 2:30pm in bad weather.

103

Val d'Isère has plenty of provision for children both on the snow and off. Depending on what you are looking for there is a nursery, an activities centre, and a variety of children-specific ski lessons.

With all facilities for children, you need to book well ahead as spaces are limited - particularly for the ski schools during the school holidays.

tour operators

Many operators offer discounted or free child places in their chalets and some packages also include free ski and boot hire, lift passes or ski lessons for children. In addition, a few operators run specific activities for children and offer chilcare. **ski scott dunn** has a huge presence in Val, and an excellent childcare programme. They run a dedicated ski school for children (aged 4-10 years) over the school holidays (Christmas/New Year, February half term and Easter), run in association with the Oxygène ski school. Children are divided into 4 different groups according to age and ability level. The company also offer private nannies to look after the children in your chalet (from 6 months aage upwards). This service must be booked before departure. **mark warner** offers a range of childcare in 3 of its 4 chalethotels (2 in Val and 1 in La Daille) for children aged 4 months-12 years. Various options are offered based on children's age and, for children over 4, skiing

104

ability. Extra babysitting services can be arranged and a member of the childcare team keep an evening watch (7:30pm-11pm) so you can enjoy your own après. **club med**, as you would expect from a leading families operator, also has a full day programme for children aged 4-10 years.

in-resort

The tourist office has a list of **babysitters**, or **serial skieur** (t 0479 416473, i serial-skieur.com) is kind of an agency for all sorts of things, including finding babysitters. Should you forget in the frenzy of packing to bring all the essentials you can rent nursery equipment from **hors-pistes** (t 0479 062869) - a little shop on left as you head into town.

A relatively new service, the **village des enfants** (t 0479 400981, e village-des-enfants@wanadoo.fr) offers a range of quality childcare options (for ages 3-8 years, Sundays-Thursdays 9am-5:30pm & Fridays 9am-2pm). These can be ski based, snow based, or simple things like painting and drama - and all classes are available in a sort of à la carte mélange that lets you choose what you want the little hobbits to do while you're off gallivanting around the ski area. Perfectly located at the Rond Point des Pistes, you can drop your children off on you way to the lifts and pick them up on your way to the bar, or wherever you might be going at the end of the day's skiing. Options include half-day, full-day and full-week supervision, with meals provided if you want them. For skiing lessons, equipment, pass and insurance are not included, so you will have to sort them out beforehand. Offering on the whole a similar service to the Village des Enfants, le **petit poucet** (t 0479 061397) covers the same age range and runs the same timetable of options for the same time every day (9am-5:30pm) - though they also have a by-the-hour service.

Most ski schools offer children's **lessons** (apart from the high-end specialist ones like Mountain Masters, Top Ski and The Development Centre). The ESF (t 0479 060234) have a comprehensive teaching programme for children, with lessons divided by age and ability level. Oxygène (t 0479 419958) have a good reputation as a children's school, and run lessons for 5-6yr olds and for children of over 6. Snowfun (t 0479 061679) run what is called the Nonours Club, which has age brackets for youngsters and also for teenagers. Evolution 2 (0479 411672) run various children's lessons which include plenty of options for the more advanced kids (both in terms of years and of ability). Snowboard specialists Billabong (t 0479 060954) also offer child-specific instruction.

Children aged 5 and under can use the **lifts** for free - though they must have a pass proving their age.

A variety of **events** and **activities** are organised throughout the season to keep smaller skiers entertained including the 'surprise' arrival of Père Nöel just before Christmas - in addition they can participate in the other activities such as ice skating and swimming. If the weather defeats best laid plans a visit to Xavier's farm (t 0479 061302) is an ideal distraction. Open Mondays, Wednesdays, Fridays and Saturdays, there are cheese-making displays and Xavier himself will give you a tour of his farm and cattle. If the lure of popcorn is more appealing, the cinema often shows a film suitable for children at 2:30pm.

105

before you go

Before you decide what kind of job you want you need to decide what kind of season you want - a job as a rep will be better paid but you have more responsibility, while a job as a chalet host means fixed hours, but once you know the routine, more time to make the most of resort life. Most of the UK ski companies recruit seasonal workers - interviewing normally starts in May, though there may still be vacancies as late as December. Either contact the companies directly (not forgetting smaller or overseas based ones)or go through a recruitment website such **natives** (i natives.co.uk) who has a comprehensive database of available jobs as well as a lot of useful information on everything about "doing a season". It's a competitive market for jobs and while it is not essential, speaking reasonable French will help. If you haven't got a job by October, it's worth going to the Ski Show at Olympia - some tour operators have a stall there as does Natives. If you haven't got a job by the start of the season, it can be worth heading out to the resort (if you can support yourself for a bit). Some of the less glamorous jobs may still be available and you will also get known - so when there is the inevitable fall-out of recruits due to unsuitability, New Year flu and mid-season blues, you can step into the role. Jobs constantly become available throughout the season - the ski market is very transient.

106

Once employed most companies organise your travel to and from the resort, accommodation, lift pass and equipment rental. Most seasonnaire jobs come with a shared room as part of the 'incentives' package. This is not true of many bar jobs - but your boss may well be able to put you in touch with someone who will help you to find somewhere to stay. If accommodation doesn't come with your job - or if you aren't planning on having a job - you would be well advised to find some digs before you head out. A group of 4 or more people should be able to find somewhere that won't break the bank. Single or double apartments are a little harder to come by, and accordingly can be pretty pricey. Be aware if you have to fork out for a season pass that they don't come cheap - but if you can prove you are working in resort for a French company the price of a season pass is hugely reduced.

once you're there

Val is a pretty intense place to work a season. It's good-time reputation is a self-fulfilling prophecy: many first-time seasonnaires go there thinking about clubbing every night rather than skiing every day - and if that's what you want it's certainly on offer. Broadly speaking, seasonnaires fall into one of two camps, skiers or drinkers - not that you can't do both, but you are likely to do significantly more of one than the other. It can appear a pretty cliquey place - again this is inevitable, as you will form a strong bond with the people you live and work with. For some this (along with the snow) is one of the main attractions of working a season. In Val it is perhaps more evident because the social scene is so non-stop - but there are a lot of seasonnaires in the valley, and the overwhelming majority are very friendly.

There are almost as many seasonnaire **hangouts** as there are bars - favourites include Pacific, the Moris, the Saloon, Bananas, the Lounge, and the Lodge. The restaurant in the Lodge is also popular, as is the Canyon, the Perdrix Blanche and Victors. Lots of the bars around town offer **seasonnaire price**s on drinks, either officially or unofficially. You're unlikely to inspire much generosity just by saying you're a seasonnaire when you order, but once people get to know your face things will likely change for the better.

Calls home are expensive from an English **mobile**, so it could be worth investing in a French SIM card - generally about £30 (of which £15 is call credit) and calls made within and out of France will be cheaper and you won't pay to receive calls from the UK. Check that your phone is 'unlocked' (so you can insert a foreign SIM card into it) before you leave the UK. You then pay as you go as you would in the UK. Top up cards are available from the various tabacs and bookshops around town. Val is one of the few places you can buy €100 top-ups - which are far

and away the most cost-effective if you're likely to use your phone a lot.

The **internet** in Val d'Isère is dominated by Powder Monkey, an English-run company who have their own internet café in the Gallerie des Cîmes, and provide the internet service in the Mountain Hub and a number of other places. There are various other options around the town as well, the cheapest of which is at Bentley's - which also has the longest hours, as the internet is available for as long as the bar is open (generally until about 1:30am).

The Val seasonnaire community is tied together by 3 main mediums of communication. **radio val** broadcasts every morning and evening in a joint English and French effort that announces things like weather forecasts and events programmes. There is an excellently unofficial resort gossip mag, called the **marmotte times**. In true seasonnaire fashion it takes the snow seriously - with features on avalanche danger and the like - and takes the partying just as seriously, keeping a regular eye on the lives of the resort's more boisterous seasonnaires, along with regular awards for the weeks silliest behaviour. Though it is a reasonably big place, Val also has a formidable **grapevine**. Do something outrageous, and your friends across town will likely know all about it before you even remember it yourself.

the a-z

tour operators

A list of the English based tour operators offering a range of accommodation in the Val d'Isère. Though many of them offer a variety of different ways to take a skiing holiday they have been categorised according to their main strength.

mainstream

airtours t 0870 238 7777,
i mytravel.com
club med t 0700 2582 932,
i clubmed.co.uk
crystal t 0870 405 5047,
i crystalski.co.uk
equity travel t 01273 886 879,
i equity.co.uk
first choice t 0870 850 3999,
i fcski.co.uk
inghams t 020 8780 4433,
i inghams.co.uk
lagrange holidays t 020 7371 6111,
i lagrange-holidays.co.uk
leisure direction t 020 8324 4042,
i leisuredirection.co.uk
lotus supertravel t 020 7295 1650,
i supertravel.co.uk
mark warner t 0870 770 4227,
i markwarner.co.uk
neilson t 0870 333 3356
i neilson.co.uk
thomson t 0870 606 1470,
i thomson-ski.co.uk

ski-specific

finlay ski t 0157 322 6611,
i finlayski.com
french life ski t 0870 197 6692,
i frenchlifeski.co.uk

handmade holidays t 01872 272 767,
i handmade-holidays.co.uk
le ski t 0870 754 4444, i leski.com
ski independence t 0870 600 1462,
i ski-independence.co.uk
rocky mountain t 0870 366 5442,
i rockymountain.co.uk
simply ski t 0208 541 2209,
i simplytravel.co.uk
silver ski t 01622 735 544,
i silverski.co.uk
ski activity t 01738 840 888,
i skiactivity.co.uk
ski beat t 01243 780 405,
i skibeat.co.uk
ski club of great britain t 020 8410 2022, i skiclub.co.uk
ski independence t 0870 600 1462,
i ski-independence.co.uk
ski supreme t 01355 260547,
i skisupreme.co.uk
ski val t 0870 746 3000, i skival.co.uk
ski world t 08702 416723,
i skiworld.ltd.uk
snowline t 0870 1123 118,
i snowline.co.uk
total t 08701 633 633, i skitotal.com

val-specific

yse t 020 8871 5117, i yseski.co.uk

luxury

descent 0207 384 3854 descent.co.uk
elegant resorts t 01244 897 333,
i elegantresorts.co.uk
VIP t 0208 875 1957, i vip-chalets.com

self-catering & budget

ams t 01743 340623, i amsrentals.com

tour operators

ski amis t 020 7692 0850, i skiamis.com
skiholidays4less t 01724 290660,
i french-freedom.co.uk
interhome t 020 8891 1294,
i interhome.co.uk
into mountains i intomountains.com
on the piste travel t 01625 503 111,
i onthepiste.co.uk
uptoyou t 0871 220 3099,
i uptoyou.com
wasteland ski & snowboard t 0906 681
8111, i wastelandski.com

self-drive
drive alive t 0114 292 2971, i drive-
alive.com
erna low t 0207 584 2841,
i ernalow.co.uk
eurotunnel motoring holidays t 0870
333 2001, i eurotunnel.com

tailor-made & weekends
alpine weekends t 0208 944 9762,
i alpineweekends.co.uk
made to measure holidays t 0124 353
3333, i madetomeasureholidays.com
momentum ski t 0207 371 9111,
i momentum.uk.com
ski scott dunn t 020 8682 5050,
i scottdunn.co.uk
ski weekend t 0870 060 0615,
i skiweekend.com
white roc ski weekends t 0207 792
1188, i whiteroc.co.uk

If you run a ski company
that offers holidays to Val d'Isère but
are not listed here, let us know by
email to comments@snowmole.com
and we will include
you in the next edition of this guide.

directory

listings

All 0450 or 06 numbers need the French international prefix (0033) if dialled from the UK.

transport

air
bmibaby t 0870 264 2229,
i bmibaby.com
british airways t 0870 850 9850,
i ba.com
easyjet t 0870 600 0000,
i easyjet.co.uk
ryanair i ryanair
swiss t 0845 601 0956, i swiss.com
chambéry t 0479 544966, i aeroport-chambery.com
geneva t 0041 22 717 7111, i gva.ch
grenoble t 0476 654848,
i grenoble.aeroport.fr
lyon t 0826 800826, i lyon.aeroport.fr
st. etienne t 0477 557171, i saint-etienne.aeroport.fr

car hire
alamo i alamo.com
avis i avis.com
(Moûtiers) t 0479 240793
easycar t 0906 333 3333
i easycar.com
europcar i europcar.com
(Bourg St. Maurice) t 0479 040420
hertz t 0870 844 8844 i hertz.co.uk
europcar france t 0479 040420
parc de voitures à val d'isère t 0479 060744

coach travel
eurolines t 08705 143219,
i nationalexpress.com

cross-channel
eurotunnel t 0870 535 3535,

directory

i eurotunnel.com
norfolkline t 01304 218400,
i norfolkline.com
speedferries t 01304 203000
i speedferries.com

driving

general - carry a valid driver's licence, proof of ownership, your insurance certificate and an emergency triangle.

petrol - there's a small petrol station as you come into town, with a small supermarket attached. For garage services go to Val d'Isère Auto Service (t 0479 412500).

speed limits - in built-up areas the speed limit is 50km/h (unless indicated). The limit is 90km/h on all other roads, 110km/h on toll-free motorways and 130km/h on toll motorways.

signs & rules - motorways in France have blue signs. Most operate a *péage* (toll) system. You must wear a seatbelt in the front and back of a car. Children under 12 must sit in the back and babies and young children must be placed in special baby/young child seats.

traffic info - (recorded) t 0826 022022

helicopter

The helipad is just past the long La Daille car park. Transfers and mountain tours available with SAF hélicoptères (t 0479 419349).

international train

raileurope t 0870 584 8848
i raileurope.co.uk
eurostar t 0870 518 6186

i eurostar.com
TGV i tgv.com

local train

SNCF t 0892 353535,
i ter-sncf.com/rhone-alpes

maps

A town map of sorts is available from the Tourist Office. For accurate backcountry navigation, the IGN 3633ET is the 1:25000 standard.

private bus

alp line t 0677 865282, i alp-line.com
alpine cab i alpinecab.com.
ats t 0709 209 7392, i a-t-s.net
mountain transfers t 07889 942786, i mountaintransfers.com

public bus

cars martin t 0479 060042
transavoie t 0479 242158, i transavoie-moutiers.com

health & safety

accidents

If you have an accident on the slopes, you will be taken to the nearest doctor unless you specify a particular one. To confirm you can pay for treatment you will need a credit card and your insurance details. At some point, contact your insurance company to check whether they want to arrange your transport home - and ask your doctor for a medical certificate confirming you are fit to travel. If you see an accident on the slopes, tell the nearest rescue centre, usually found at the top or bottom of lifts.

doctors

Two choices in the centre of town, both of which are English speaking:
du Centre medical centre t 0479 060611, du Val Village medical centre t 0479 061370. There is a slightly larger outfit at the north end of town, by the large pharmacy past Simon's Café: MédiVal medical centre t 0479 402680

emergency numbers

fire service t 18 or t 0479 060180
medical emergencies t 15 or t 112
gendarmerie t 17 or t 0479 060341
police municipale t 0479 061096
piste security t 0479 060210
ambulance t 0479 064300

health

An E111 form (available from any UK post office) entitles you to treatment under the French health system. While you have to pay for your treatment when you receive it, you can then get a refund for up to 70% of medical expenses - as long as you keep all your receipts.

insurance

It is essential to have personal insurance covering wintersports and the cost of any ambulances, helicopter rescue and emergency repatriation - all these services are very expensive. Insurance policies differ greatly - some exclude off-piste skiing or cover it only if you are with a guide, so you need to check the terms and conditions carefully.

pharmacies

Pharmacie du Village t 0479 062610 or Pharmacie du Solaise t 0601 68

physiotherapists

For your aches and pains there are a number of physio centres including MédiVal t 0479 065274 and Bonne Santé t 0479 060727.

safety on the mountain

avalanche danger - the risk of avalanche is graded from 1 to 5.
1 & 2. (yellow) low risk.
3 & 4. (checked yellow and black) moderate risk, caution advised when skiing off-piste
5. (black) high risk, off-piste skiing strongly discouraged.
The risk is displayed on a flag at the main lift stations, but if you are in any

doubt about where it is safe to ski, ask the advice of the lift operators.

food & drink - a skiing holiday is not the time to start a diet. Your body expends energy keeping warm and exercising so it's a good idea to eat a decent breakfast, and carry some chocolate or sweets with you.

The body dehydrates more quickly at altitude and whilst exercising. You need to drink a lot (of water) each day to replace the moisture you lose.

rules of conduct - the International Ski Federation publishes conduct rules for all skiers and boarders:

1. respect - do not endanger or prejudice others.

2. control - ski in control, adapting speed and manner to ability, the conditions and the traffic.

3. choice of route - the uphill skier must choose his route so he does not endanger skiers ahead.

4. overtaking - allowed above or below, right or left, but leave enough room for the overtaken skier.

5. entering & starting a run - look up and down the piste when doing so.

6. stopping on the piste - avoid stopping in narrow places or where visibility is restricted.

7. climbing - keep to the side of the piste when climbing up or down.

8. signs & markings - respect these.

9. assistance - every skier must assist at accidents.

10. identification - all involved in an accident (including witnesses) must exchange details.

snow & avalanche information
t 0892 681020

weather
Daily updates t 0892 680273 (French), i meteo.fr. The daily forecast is posted outside the tourist office at 8:30am and 6pm or Henry's avalanche report in the Marmotte Times.

what to wear
Several, thin layers are better than one thick piece. Avoid cotton, which keeps moisture next to the body, so cooling it down. A windproof and waterproof material (such as Goretex) is best for outer layers. A hat is essential to keep you warm and protect the scalp from sunburn as are gloves to keep hands warm. Sunglasses or goggles are essential. Wrap-arounds are a good choice and lenses should be shatter-proof and give 100% protection from UVA and UVB rays. Poor eye protection can lead to snowblindness, which makes the eyes water and feel painful and gritty. Treat by resting eyes in a darkened room, and applying cold compresses. You should wear UVA and UVB sun protection with a high factor (SPF) at all times, even if overcast and cloudy. The sun is more intense at higher altitude, so you should re-apply regularly (particularly after falling or sweating). Don't forget to cover your ear lobes and the underside of the nose.

directory

resort survival

banks & atms

There are surprisingly few ATMs in town - you may find yourself standing in line to get at your cash, much in the same way as you will then be standing in line to spend your money in the bar. There are 4 banks - 3 of which close all weekend: Banque Populaire (t 0820 337972), Banque de Savoie (t 0479 060165) and Lyonnaise de Banque (t 0820 010102). Crédit Agricole (t 0479 060163) is only closed on Sunday. Each of these has an ATM, and there is a fifth at the post office.

conference center

If you're missing job - or your bringing it with you - the Henri Oreiller centre up by the Barmes de l'Ours hotel, has full conference facilities, including 9 conference rooms, a 650 sq. meter function room, and 130 underground parking spaces (t 0479 062123, i valdisere-congres.com)

church services

The lovely old church in the Vieux Village (t 0479 060528) has services on Saturdays at 6pm and Sundays at 9:30am.

dvds & videos

In the centre of Val, try Val Menager du Carouge (t 0479 060564) or Video Val (t 0479 419728) or the Phillips shop next to Ski Mastery. Further out is Val net/L'Avalin services (t 0479 412574/0479 401753 - out towards Le Crêt)

haircuts

For a Toni & Guy cut, head to La Coupe behind the Grand Paradis hotel (t 0479 060492). For a Nicki Clarke experience, Paul Berrard is a beauty salon with full hair facilities. For economy and convenience, Helen Mobile Hairdressing (t 0699 736072) is based in La Daille but will come to wherever you are.

internet/email

ADSL broadband is forecast to arrive in time for the 04-05 season - though it is unlikely to be either widespread or even fully functional until somewhat later. There are a number of internet options in town, the standard being Powder Monkey, which runs a 'café' in the Gallerie des Cimes and the internet end of the Mountain Hub. There is also reliable and slightly less expensive email in the Lounge and Bentley's bars - Bentley's service runs through until the bar closes at 1:30am.

laundry & dry cleaning

There are 4 automated laundry services in town: Le Portillo (t 0622 730531) and Grand Lessive (t 0479 060167) are central and quite pricey. Lav d'Isère (t 0479 062608) and Lavomatique du Vieux Village (t 0479 412574) are less expensive but further out from the middle of town.

directory

lift pass company

The STVI (Société des Téléphériques de Val d'Isère) is based up at the Rond-Point, in the same building as the Soliase Cable Car. Relations with the Tourist Office are not as amicable as they could be, but

market

Val has a Monday market around the centre of town and up to the front de neige. A lot of the shops close on Mondays as a result, particularly around the area of the market stalls. There are a disproportionate number sweets and sausages, along with generally poor quality winter clothing.

newspapers

All the *Presse* shops in town sell English newspapaers.

parking

There is very limited street-side parking in the town. The back road that runs parallel to the main street sometimes has spaces at the northern end, but generally if you want to park in town you should use the underground parking. Prices are very reasonable compared to English pay & display. If you park illegally you will usually get a warning first time around, but if you just stick car somewhere and leave it for a week it is liable to be towed. The car pound number is t 0479 061096.

passport photos

There's a photo machine in the main lift pass office by the crêperie Grand Marnier, and also one in Hervé, a small shop opposite Crêpe Val's.

police

The Police Municipale are based at the north end of town, though if you need a policeman they are most easily found wandering the streets dishing out warning tickets to illegally parked cars.

post

The post office (t 0479 060699) is open 9am-5:30pm on weekdays and 8:30am-11:30am on Saturdays.

radio stations

Run out of the Tourist Office, Radio Val d'Isère 96.1FM broadcasts in English morning and evening.

shopping

Most shops open every day (except public holidays) 8:30am-12:30pm and 2:30pm-7pm.

supermarkets - Val has 3 main supermarkets - 2 Spars and a Sherpa, not that there's a great deal of difference between them. The first 2 are at the first roundabout in town, 1 on either side of the road, and the third is just out of the far end of town heading towards Le Laisinant. If you're on your way out of town and want to stock up on basics there is also small Spar at the petrol station. Along with baguettes and cheese and sausages, you can also buy a number of English favourites like Marmite and Baked Beans - though if beans means Heinz then it also means paying about 5 times what you would normally spend. If you are driving to resort your best bet is to stock up before heading up the mountain. There is a large supermarket just past Albertville on the way in, and another in Bourg St. Maurice where there is also a Lidl for very cheap wine.

local produce - for more specialist shopping there are a handful of shops that sell regional produce, including a nice but pricey wine shop opposite the tourist office - for cheaper options try Lidl in Bourg St. Maurice. You can also get local produce at the market.

clothes - the larger ski shops stock various brands, but generally the choice is pretty samey wherever you go.

ski & board servicing

The best ski servicing in town is provided by 3 Wintersteiger machines (of which there are only 4 in Europe) run by SnowTec. SnowTec is behind both Precision and SnowFun, and you can generally get an overnight service from either establishment. Killy Sport and Ogier also have provide quality servicing. For boarders, though anywhere can chuck some wax on a plank of wood, to be sure of a decent edging service or any kind of serious recovery, you are best off at Misty Fly (or Precision again).

taxis

bozzetto t 0479 060250
abc taxis t 0479 061992

taxi nicolas t 0479 410125
altitude espace taxi t 0607 411153
taxi papillon t 0608 999396
aa taxi t 0479 060295/0609 519099
inter service savoie t 0607 950538
aiglon taxi t 0479 075857/0611 339127

tourist offices

Val d'Isère's main tourist office (t 0479 060660) is located at the heart of the resort, open daily 8:30am-7:30pm except Saturdays when it is open until 8pm.

In La Daille tourist information can be obtained from the Chalet D'Information.

websites

Val d'Isère's official website (i valdisere.com) is very good. It has an English option, and provides good information on the ski area along with allowing you to book accommodation online. The unofficial version, valdinet.com, is aimed more specifically at the English market and is a better place to find out the realities of the resort along with finding links to English tour operators and other relevant companies.

directory

country survival

customs
As France is part of the EU, there are few restrictions on what UK visitors can take out for personal use.

electricity
220 volts/50hz ac. Appliances use a two-pin plug - adaptors are readily available form electrical stores or supermarkets.

language
Officially French but most places more English than anything else.

money
The currency is the Euro (€). €1 is equivalent to 100 centimes. Notes come in anything from €10 to €500. You can exchange money in the banks in La Plagne during the week, and also at the airports and in major train stations. In 2004, the average exchange rate for UK£1 = (approx) €1.6

public holidays
December   6 - St Nicholas Day
                 25 - Christmas Day
                 26 - St Stephen's day
January   1 - New Year's Day
March/April Good Friday, Easter
Sunday & Monday

telephone
Public phones boxes are located throughout the town and accept coins or phonecards, which can be bought from the post office, tabacs, and train and petrol stations. All local and calls within Europe are cheaper 7pm-8am during the week and all day at the weekend. The international dialling code for France is 0033; the free international operator t 12; the international directory information t 1159; and national directory information t 111. There are 3 mobile phone networks: Bouyges Telecom, France telecom/Orange and SFR.

time
France is always one hour ahead of England.

tipping
All food bills include a service charge, though it is common to make an addition for drinks or for noticeably good service.

water
Tap water is drinkable, except where there is an eau non potable sign.

glossary

a

arête - a sharp ridge.

avalanche - a rapid slide of snow down a slope.

avalanche transceiver - a device used when skiing off-piste, which can both emit and track a high frequency signal to allow skiers lost in an avalanche or a crevasse to be found.

b

BASI - British Association of Snowsport Instructors.

binding - attaches boot to ski.

black run/piste - difficult, generally steeper than a red piste.

blood wagon - a stretcher on runners used by ski patrollers to carry injured skiers off the mountain.

blue run/piste - easy, generally wide with a gentle slope.

bubble ➙ 'gondola'.

button (or Poma) lift - for 1 person. Skis and boards run along the ground, whilst you sit on a small 'button' shaped seat.

c

cable car - a large box-shaped lift, running on a thick cable over pylons high above the ground, which carry up to 250 people per car.

carving - a recently developed turning technique used by skiers and boarders to make big, sweeping turns across the piste.

carving skis - shorter and fatter than traditional skis, used for carving turns.

chairlift - like a small and uncomfortable sofa, which scoops you and your skis off the ground and carries you up the mountain. Once on, a protective bar with a rest for your skis holds you in place. Can carry 2-6 people.

couloir - a 'corridor' between 2 ridges, normally steep and narrow.

crampons - spiked fittings attached to outdoor or ski boots to climb mountains or walk on ice.

d

draglift or (T-bar) - for 2 people. Skis and boards run on the ground, whilst you lean against a small bar.

drop-off - a sharp increase in gradient.

e

edge - the metal ridge on the border of each side of the ski.

f

FIS - Federation Internationale du Ski.

flat light - lack of contrast caused by shadow or cloud, making it very difficult to judge depth and distance.

freeriding, freeskiing - off-piste skiing.

freestyle - skiing involving jumps.

g

glacier - a slow-moving ice mass formed thousands of years ago and fed each year by fresh snow.

gondola (or bubble) - an enclosed lift, often with seats.

h

heliskiing - off-piste skiing on routes only accessible by helicopter.

high season - weeks when the resort is (generally) at full capacity.

i

itinerary route (yellow) - not groomed, maintained or patrolled.

Generally more difficult, at least in part, than a black piste. Can be skied without a guide.

k

kicker - jump.

l

lambchop drag ➥ 'rope tow'.

ledgy - off-piste conditions in which there are many short, sharp drop-offs.

low season - beginning and end of the season and the least popular weeks in mid-January.

m

mid season - reasonably popular weeks in which the resort is busy but not full.

mogul - a bump, small or large, on or off piste. A large mogulled area is called a mogul field.

o

off-piste - the area away from marked, prepared and patrolled pistes.

p

parallel turn - skis turn in parallel.

piste - a ski run marked, groomed and patrolled, and graded in terms of difficulty (blue, red or black).

piste basher - a bulldozer designed to groom pistes by smoothing snow.

pisteur - a ski piste patroller.

Poma ➥ 'button lift'.

powder - fresh, unbashed or untracked snow.

r

raquettes ➥ 'snowshoes'.

red run/piste - intermediate, normally steeper than a blue piste, although a flatish piste may be a red because it is narrow, has a steep drop-off or because snow conditions are worse than on other pistes.

rope tow (or lambchop drag) - a constantly moving loop of rope with small handles to grab onto to take you up a slope.

s

schuss - a straight slope down which you can ski very fast.

seasonnaire - an individual who lives (and usually works) in a ski resort for the season.

skis - technology has changed in the last 10 years. New skis are now shorter and wider. When renting, you will be given a pair approx. 5-10cms shorter than your height.

ski patrol - a team of piste patrollers

skins - artificial fur attached to ski base, for ski touring.

snow-chains - chains attached to car tyres so that it can be driven (cautiously) over snow or ice.

snowshoes - footwear resembling tennis rackets which attach to shoes, for walking on soft snow.

spring snow - granular, heavy snow conditions common in late season (when daytime temperatures rise causing snow to thaw and re-freeze).

steeps - a slope with a very steep gradient.

t

T-bar ➥ 'draglift'.

w

white-out - complete lack of visibility caused by enveloping cloud cover.

index

index

further information

also available the snowmole guides to...
france
chamonix mont-blanc
courchevel les 3 vallées
la plagne paradiski
les arcs paradiski
méribel les 3 vallées
switzerland
verbier val de bagnes
zermatt matterhorn

coming soon the snowmole guides to...
st. anton arlberg
davos
tignes espace killy
ski weekends

also the underground network

accuracy & updates

We have tried our best to ensure that all the information included is accurate at the date of publication. However, because places change - improve, get worse, or even close - you may find things different when you get there. Also, everybody's experience is different and you may not agree with our opinion. You can help us, in 2 ways: by letting us know of any changes you notice and by telling us what you think - good or bad - about what we've written. If you have any comments, ideas or suggestions, please write to us at: snowmole, 45 Mysore Road, London, SW11 5RY or send an email to comments@snowmole.com

snowmole.com

Our website is intended as a compliment to our guides. Constantly evolving and frequently updated with news, you will find links to other wintersport related websites, information on our stockists and offers and the latest news about future editions and new titles. We also use our website to let you know of any major changes that occur after we publish the guides. If you would like to receive news and updates about our books by email, please register your details at www.snowmole.com

order form

The snowmole guides are available from all major bookshops, wintersports retailers or direct from Qanuk Publishing & Design Ltd. To experience the Alps without leaving home have your next snowmole guide delivered to your door. To order send an email to sales@snowmole.com or fill in the form below and send it to us at Qanuk Publishing & Design Ltd, 45 Mysore Road, London, SW11 5RY

the snowmole guide to:	ISBN	quantity
chamonix mont blanc	0-9545739-3-5	----------------------------
courchevel les 3 vallées	0-9545739-5-1	----------------------------
la plagne paradiski	0-9545739-8-6	----------------------------
les arcs paradiski	0-9545739-7-8	----------------------------
méribel les 3 vallées	0-9545739-4-3	----------------------------
val d'isère espace killy	0-9545739-9-4	----------------------------
verbier val de bagnes	0-9545739-2-7	----------------------------
zermatt matterhorn	0-9545739-6-X	----------------------------

total: ----------------------------
(£6.99 each, postage & packaging free)

I enclose a cheque for £
(made payable to Qanuk Publishing & Design Ltd)

name ---
address ---
postcode ---
tel--
email address--
(please use block capitals)

Delivery will normally be within 14 working days. The availability and published prices quoted are correct at the time of going to press but are subject to alteration without prior notice. Please note that this service is only available in the UK.

Qanuk would like to keep you updated on new titles in the snowmole range or special offers. If you do not wish to receive such information please tick here ☐
Qanuk has a number of partners in the ski industry, and we may from time to time share your details with those partners if we think it might be of interest to you. If you do not wish us to share your details please tick here ☐

about you

Your comments, opinions and recommendations are very important to us. To help us improve the snowmole guides, please take a few minutes to complete this short questionnaire. Once completed please send it to us at Qanuk Publishing & Design Ltd.

name (Mr/Mrs/Ms) --
address ---
postcode ---
email address --
age ---
occupation ---

1. about your ski holiday (circle as appropriate)
how many days do you ski each year?
weekend/1 week/2 weeks/1 month/more
when do you book?
last-minute/1 month before/1-3 months before/3-6 months before
how do you book your holiday?
travel agent/mainstream tour operator/ski-specific tour operator/diy

2. about the snowmole guide
which title did you buy?---
where and when did you buy it?--
have you bought any other snowmole guides?------------------------------
if so, which one(s) ---
how would you rate each section out of 5 (1 = useless, 5 = very useful)
getting started --
the skiing --
the resort --
the directory --
the maps ---
what in particular made you buy this guide?-------------------------------
----
do you have any general comments or suggestions?-----------------------
----
did you buy any other guides for your holiday? --------------------------
if yes, which one? ---
Qanuk Publishing & Design Ltd may use information about you to provide you with details of other products and services, by telephone, email or in writing. If you do not wish to receive such details please tick here ☐

about us

snowmole / snṓmōl / n. & v. **1** a spy operating within alpine territory (esp. ski resorts) for the purpose of gathering local knowledge. **2** (in full **snowmole guide**) the guidebook containing information so gathered. v. research or compile or process intelligence on an alpine resort or surrounding mountainous area.

the authors
Isobel Rostron and Michael Kayson are snowsport enthusiasts who met while taking time out from real life to indulge their passion - Isobel to get it out of her system and Michael to ingrain it further. Michael's approach having won, they decided that a return to real life was overrated and came up with a cunning plan to make their passion their work. The result was snowmole.

acknowledgments & credits
None of this would have been possible without the help and support of many people:
Antonia Lee-Bapty, Dougie Cleland, Danni Hayes, Phil Lorraines, Paul Nawano, Ellie Martin-Sperry, Andrew Lilley for his invaluable and underpaid proofreading skills, Angela Horne, Julian Horne, Maisie, Christine & Peter Rostron and Tom, Henry, Katie Fyson for their ongoing support.

The publishers would like to thank the following for their kind permission to reproduce their photographs.
front cover: Office de Tourisme de Val d'Isère
back cover: Office de Tourisme de Courchevel 1850 & Office de Tourisme de La Plagne
inside: title page and pages 10, 12, 14, 15, 72 and 73 Office de Tourisme de Val d'Isère.
The remaining photographs are held in the publisher's own photo library and were taken by Isobel Rostron.

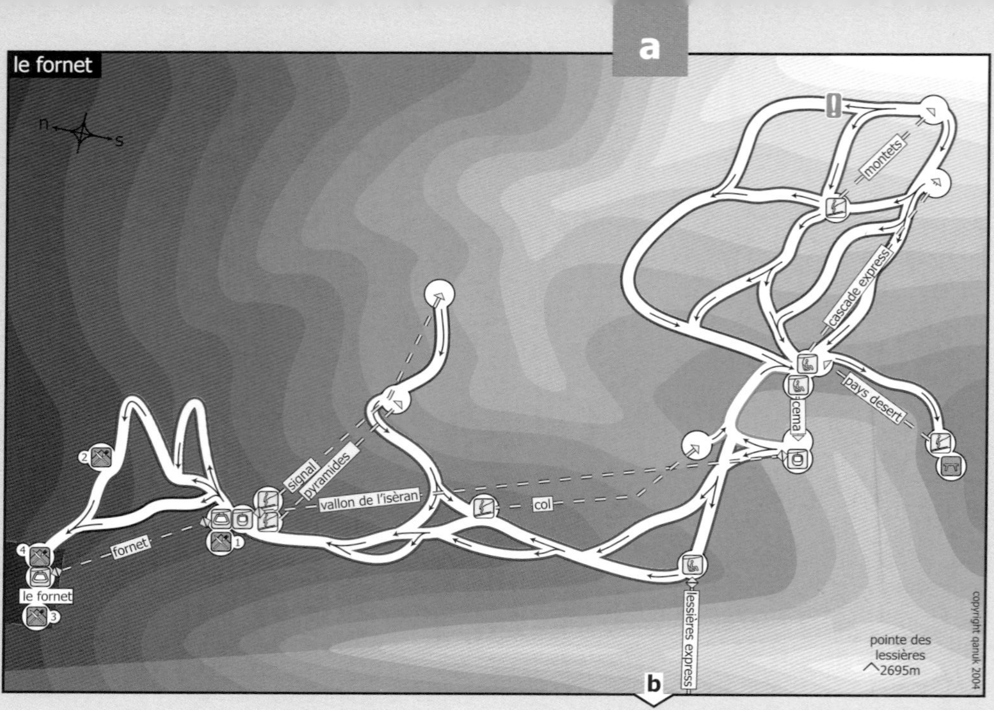
le fornet
a
n
s
montets
cascade express
pays desert
cema
signal
pyramides
vallon de l'isèran
col
fornet
le fornet
1
2
3
4
lessières express
b
pointe des
lessières
2695m
copyright qanuk 2004

le fornet

le fornet

		🕐	pistes	queues	moguls I II III IIII	off-piste I II III IIII
fornet	80	3m30		≋≋≋≋		●
i vallon de l'iséran	6	12m10		≋≋		●
signal	1	8m15		≋		● ●
pyramides	1	5m35		≋		●
col	1	5m00				●
cema	4	4m00		≋		●
i pays desert	1	2m10				●
cascade express	4	6m10		≋	●	●
i montets	2	5m10		≋		●
i lessières express	6	4m10		≋		●

i
vallon de l'iséran	doors sometimes don't close fully (!)
pays desert	return from a number of off-piste routes
montets	glacier skiing - off-piste is crevassed
lessières express	access solaise sector - return to val d'isère

1	le signal
2	edelweiss
3	l'arolay
4	les crozets

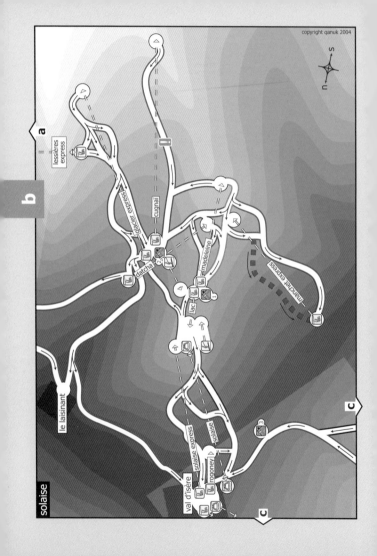

solaise

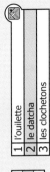

solaise

	⏱	pistes	queues	moguls I II III IIII	off-piste I II III IIII
solaise express	🚡 4	8m30	■ ※※ 1		●
rogoney	🚡 4	4m30	※※ 1	●	● ●
solaise	🚡 80	6m10	■ ※※ 1		● ● ●
lac	🚡 4	2m10	※※		
madeleine	🚡 4	6m30	※※	●	● ● ●
datcha	🚡 3	6m10	※※	●	●
glacier express	🚡 6	7m30	※※		● ●
cugnaï	🚡 2	15m10	※		● ● ●
lessières express	🚡 6	4m10	※		● ●
manchet express	🚡 4	7m20			● ●

ℹ️ rogoney — stays open in most bad weather
cugnaï — long and very slow
lessières express — access to le fornet sector

1 l'ouilette
2 le datcha
3 les clochetons

b

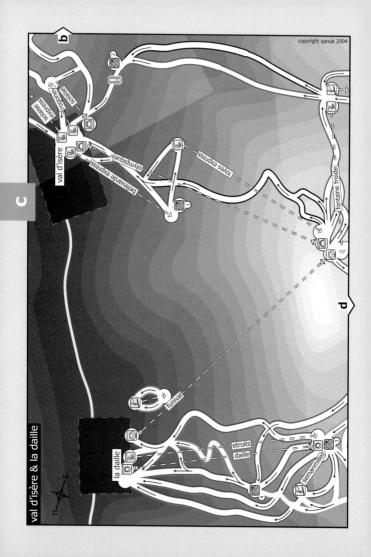

val d'isère & la daille

copyright ganuk 2004

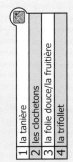

val d'isère & la daille

val d'isère & la daille

		⏱	pistes	queues	moguls I II III	off-piste I II III
olympique	30	9m45				
bellevarde express	4	4m40				
loyes express	4	6m20				
fontaine froide	3	8m45				
funival	80	5m40				
etroits	3	12m30				
daille	4	8m30				
semanmille	1	6m00				

olympique — the queue moves pretty quickly, but at peak times it is much faster to take the bellevarde express and the loyes express chairlifts

etroits — this is the quickest route into the bellevarde area from la daille at peak times

1 la tanière
2 les clochetons
3 la folie douce/la fruitière
4 la trifollet

bellevarde

rocher du charvet
2856m

grand pré

santons

fontaine froide

olympique

lloyes express

funival

marmottes

dorsat express

tessa

mont blanc

snowpark

slalom

tommeuses

tufs

aerosol

copyright qanuk 2004

bellevarde

bellevarde

			pistes	queues	moguls			off-piste		
		⏱			I | II | III		I | II | III	
	marmottes	🚡3	9m30	■ ■ ■	≋≋				●	
ⓘ	borsat express	🚡4	8m45	■ ■	≋≋				●	
ⓘ	mont blanc	🚡3	9m00	■	≋				●	
ⓘ	tommeuses	🚡8	6m40	■ ■	≋≋		● ●		●	●
	fontaine froide	🚡4	8m45	■ ■	≋≋		●		●	
	santons	🚡1	4m00	■ ■					●	
ⓘ	grand pré	🚡4	6m15	■ ■	≋≋					●
ⓘ	slalom	🚡1	2m50	■ ■	≋≋					
ⓘ	snowpark	🚡1	2m50	■	≋					

ⓘ
tommeuses	tignes access
borsat express	alternative tignes access (val claret only)
grand pré	access to the start of the tour du charvet
slalom/snowpark	snowpark access
mont blanc	snowpark access

🚡
1	bellevarde
2	les marmottes
3	la folie douce/la fruitière
4	la tovière

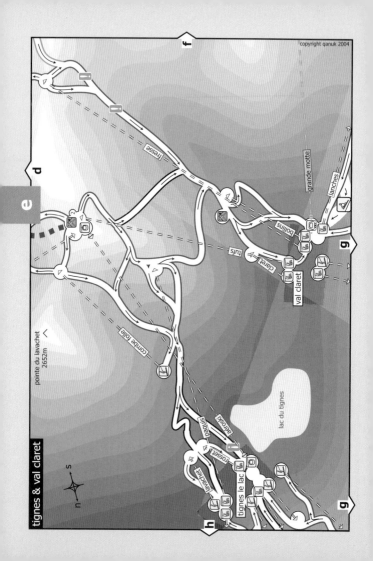

tignes & val claret

copyright qanuk 2004

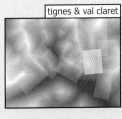

tignes & val claret

1 | la tovière

tignes & val claret

	⏱	pistes	queues	moguls I II III	off-piste I II III
bollins 🚡4	3m10		🎿🎿🎿		
fresse 🚡4	11m50		🎿🎿🎿 !	● ●	● ●
tufs 🚡3	12m00	■	🎿🎿🎿 !		● ●
claret 🚡3	3m00		🎿		
aéroski 🚠10	8m20	■	🎿🎿🎿	● ●	● ●
rosset 🚡3	3m20	■	🎿		
paquis 🚡6	7m25	■	🎿🎿🎿	● ●	● ●
lavachet 🚡1	2m30	■	🎿		
combe folle 🚡1	4m30	■		● ●	● ●

ⓘ		
bollin/fresse	the lifts alternate on the same cables - make sure you're in the right queue: the fresse is the direct return for val d'isère, or you can take the bollins & ski down to the tufs chairlift	
tufs	return to val d'isère	
aéroski	return to val d'isère	
paquis	alternative return to val d'isère with combe folle	

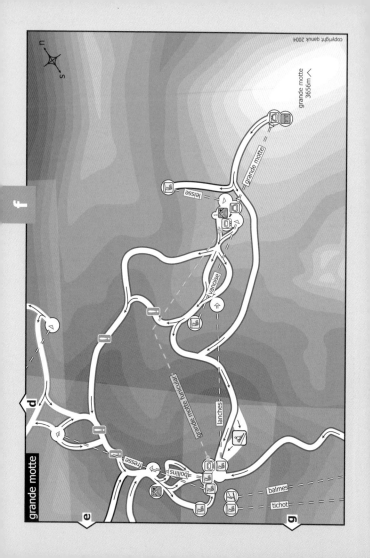

grande motte
3656m

grande motte

copyright danuk 2004

leisse

vanoise

grande motte funicula

lanches

tresse

bollins

balmes

tichot

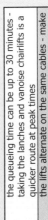

grande motte

1 | le panoramic

grande motte

		⏱	pistes	queues	moguls I	II	III	off-piste I	II	III
i funicular	🚡80	8m00	■	⛷⛷ ①				●		
lanches	🚡4	9m20	■ ■	⛷				●		
vanoise	🚡4	5m00	■	⛷				●		
grande motte	🚡120	5m00	■	⛷⛷ ①			●	●	●	
leisse	🚡4	6m30	■ ■	⛷⛷				●		
i bollins	🚡4	3m10	■ ■	⛷⛷				●		
i fresse	🚡4	11m50	■	⛷⛷ ①				●		

i funicular	the queueing time can be up to 30 minutes - taking the lanches and vanoise chairlifts is a quicker route at peak times
bollins/fresse	the lifts alternate on the same cables - make sure you're in the right queue: the fresse is the direct return for val d'isère, or you can take the bollins and ski down to the tufs chairlift

f

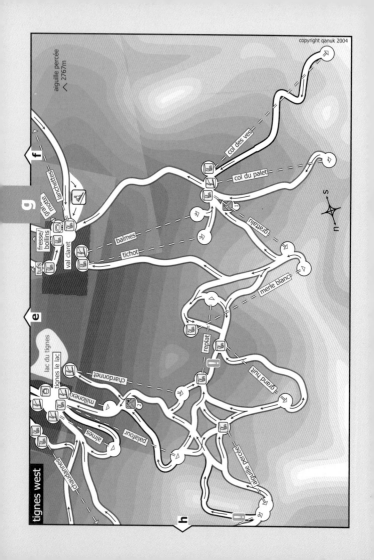

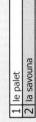

tigns west

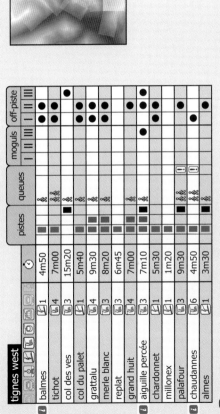

tignes west

		⏱	pistes	queues	moguls I II III	off-piste I II III
i balmes	☂1	4m50				
tichot	☂4	7m00				
col des ves	☂3	15m20				
col du palet	☂1	5m40				
grattalu	☂4	9m30				
merle blanc	☂3	8m20				
replat	☂3	6m45				
grand huit	☂4	7m00				
i aiguille percée	☂3	7m10				
chardonnet	☂1	5m30				
millonex	☂1	1m20				
palafour	☂3	9m30				
i chaudannes	☂6	4m50				
almes	☂1	3m30				

i balmes — téléski difficile
aiguille percée — access les brevières
chaudannes — access les brevières

1 le palet
2 la savouna

9

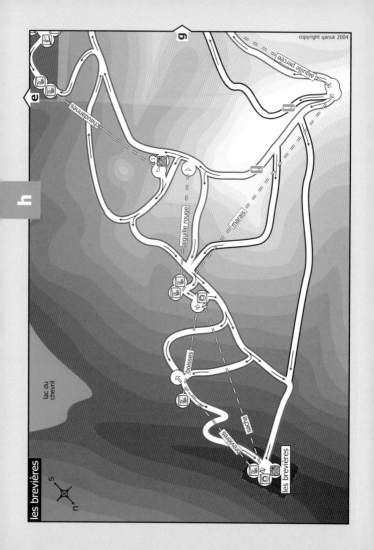

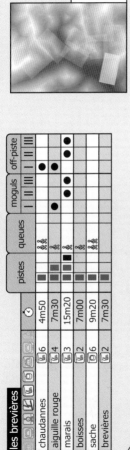

les brevières

1 l'alpage

les brevières

		⏱	pistes	queues	moguls I II III	off-piste I II III
chaudannes	🚡6	4m50				
aiguille rouge	🚡4	7m30			●	
marais	🚡3	15m20			●	
boisses	🚡2	7m00				●
sache	🚡6	9m20				●
brevières	🚡2	7m30				

ⓘ aiguille rouge — return to tignes & val d'isère
marais — long and slow - best avoided in cold weather

◇ ski area key

val d'isère
a - le fornet
b - solaise
c - val & la daille
d - bellevarde

tignes
e - tignes & val claret
f - grande motte
g - tignes west
h - les brevières

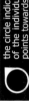

the circle indicates the page orientation of the individual ski maps - the arrow points towards the top of the page